GOD OF OUR
FATHERS

GOD OF OUR FATHERS

An anthology of British prayers
through the centuries

COMPILED AND EDITED
BY
FRANK COLQUHOUN

Hodder & Stoughton
LONDON SYDNEY AUCKLAND TORONTO

British Library Cataloguing in Publication Data
God of our fathers.
  1. Christian life. Prayers. Devotional works
  I. Colquhoun, Frank
  242.8

ISBN 0-340-52937-7

First published in Great Britain 1990

Published by Hodder and Stoughton,
a division of Hodder and Stoughton Ltd,
Mill Road, Dunton Green, Sevenoaks, Kent TN13 2YA
Editorial Office: 47 Bedford Square, London WC1B 3DP

Photoset by Rowland Phototypesetting Ltd,
Bury St Edmunds, Suffolk

Printed in Great Britain by Clays Ltd, St Ives plc

Contents

Foreword   7

Editor's Introduction   9

I   THE EARLY CENTURIES   15

    Sectional prayers:
      Prayers of the Celtic tradition   34

II THE REFORMATION AND ELIZABETHAN
    PERIOD   41

    Sectional prayers:
      Prayers of the Protestant
      Reformers   47
      The Book of Common Prayer,
      1549, 1552, 1559   53
      General prayers of the Elizabethan
      era   65

III THE SEVENTEENTH AND EIGHTEENTH
    CENTURIES   75

    Sectional prayers:
      Prayers of Bishop Lancelot
      Andrewes   80
      The Book of Common Prayer,
      1662   86

Prayers of Bishop Jeremy Taylor   95
Prayers of famous men and
women of the period   102
Prayers of the poets of the period   118

IV   THE GEORGIAN AND VICTORIAN AGE   127

Sectional prayers:
Prayers of famous men and
women of the period   138
Prayers of Victorian
hymn-writers   151
Prayers of the poets of the period   162
Prayers of Bishop Brooke Foss
Westcott   172

V   THE TWENTIETH CENTURY   175

Sectional prayers:
Prayers of the Proposed Prayer
Book, 1928   186
War-time prayers of 1914–18 and
1939–45   198
Prayers of Archbishop William
Temple   206
Prayers of the Scottish Churches   222
Prayers of the Church of Ireland   226
Welsh prayers of the century   229

Acknowledgments   233
Index of Sources   235
Index of Subjects   238

Foreword

I am deeply grateful to Canon Frank Colquhoun for allowing me to see this exceptional collection of prayers, which must have taken him years of patient search, joyful discovery, and helpful arrangement. I have read every single one, lingering over many which were relevant to my own devotional needs. A number of them were already known to me, while others were new. It is particularly good to see, here and there, prayers written and prayed by Frank himself.

The idea of what might be called a prayer history of the British people was first suggested by the late Eric Milner-White, Dean of King's College, Cambridge, and then Dean of York, and if those in God's new order of spirituality and eternity are allowed in the divine providence to know something of what is happening among those of us still in the preparatory school of human life, Dean Eric will be thanking God for Canon Frank.

In this comprehensive collection will be found prayers by British monarchs, statesmen, theologians, poets and historical figures of almost every generation of Christians. In many cases, the historical concerns expressed in the individual prayers arise from the historical situations in which they were written. The introduction sketches in the historical background to the five sections in a way that greatly assists in the understanding of each prayer. I was particularly pleased to see Nelson's prayer before Trafalgar (No. 251), my favourite hymn of

Charles Wesley 'O Thou who camest from above' (No. 228), the moving prayer of Thomas More, prayed a few days before his execution (No. 57), Dr Pusey's prayer 'Let us never seek *out* of thee what we can find only *in* thee' (No. 240), Christina Rossetti's 'None other Lamb' (No. 302). Among new ones to me was Professor Knight's challenging one on jealousy (No. 295), and I found myself saying 'amen' to Archbishop Benson's prayer 'Teach me, good Lord, not to murmur at multitude of business or shortness of time' (and the slow-down of old age) (No. 272).

This treasury of Christian devotion will be invaluable for parish clergy and for all who conduct Christian worship.

Bishop George Appleton

Editor's Introduction

'The World will be saved by only one thing and that is worship.' So wrote Archbishop William Temple. By worship he doubtless meant man's recognition of God's sovereign claims and giving him his due glory.

Prayer is the central part of worship, and the prayers in this book are essentially acts of worship. That at once establishes something of their worth.

The distinctive feature of the prayers is that they are all of British origin, representative of the English, Scottish, Irish and Welsh traditions. Accordingly they go back to Patrick and Columba, Bede and Alfred, and continue through succeeding centuries to the present day. The prayers thus reflect something of the history of the British people, and many of them are written by leading figures both in Church and State.

Inevitably the majority of them are of English origin. It is those prayers that have been principally preserved in the national archives and are therefore most readily accessible. Many are well known and have long been in general use; but certainly some will be 'new' and unfamiliar to the average worshipper.

It will be clear enough that the material is divided into five historical parts. These cover in turn the early centuries as far as the fifteenth and include some Celtic prayers; the sixteenth century follows, with its prayers of the Reformation and Elizabethan age; next are the prayers of the seventeenth and eighteenth centuries; and so to the previous century, with its abundant choice of Victorian prayers; and lastly prayers of the present century, also plentiful enough.

In the first part, the earliest prayers selected are those which have survived from the Celtic Church in Britain – from the period before St Augustine came from Rome to be the first Archbishop of Canterbury. These Celtic (or Gaelic) prayers are characterised by a complete openness to God. They see and seek his presence in the ordinary, daily, commonplace things of life, while at the same time acknowledging the glory of the Eternal Trinity.

As the Roman Church extended its influence in Britain, it brought both leadership and organisation to what had been the small and rather scattered Celtic Church. The growing number of bishops is represented by some of their prayers in this part. These leaders of the British Church were not always scholars, but were certainly men of real Christian devotion and vision. These elements are very obvious in their prayers.

The first part also includes the beginning, with King Alfred, of the long tradition of prayers by British sovereigns.

In Part II, one of the most profound influences on the British Church – the Reformation – is reflected in the authors of the prayers and the nature of their spirituality.

The second significant factor in the period was the publication of the Book of Common Prayer. The break with the papacy and subsequent abandonment of the Roman Mass required a new manual of worship and devotion. In compiling the book, Archbishop Cranmer aimed to provide services that were simple, intelligible and scriptural. His resolve that 'Now from henceforth the whole Realm shall have but one use' resulted in a prayer book *common* to the whole English Church. And while the book is essentially of English origin, its forms of worship were widely adopted by the Anglican Churches of Ireland, Scotland and Wales. The selection of prayers in Part II is representative of Cranmer's masterpiece, which through the years has exerted a profound influence on the life of the British people.

The seventeenth and eighteenth centuries, which are the basis for Part III, saw both the translation of the Authorised, or King James, Version of the Bible, 1611, and later, the outbreak of the English Revolution. One of the translators of the Authorised Version was Lancelot Andrewes, Bishop of Chichester and then of Winchester. Andrewes is typical of the devout scholastic bishops of the Church of England, and his prayers, originally written for his private use, are masterpieces of devotional writing.

With the coming to power of the Puritans, the National Church as such ceased to exist, and very few prayers of this period survive. There is a similar lack of surviving prayers from the eighteenth century, though for different reasons. The prayers from the period covered in Part III vary in style and language, but exhibit a common factor in their approach to God in a spirit of reverence, devotion, penitence and praise.

The fourth part covers the nineteenth century with the Victorian revival of family prayers in middle-class Christian households. This gave rise to the publication of numerous prayer manuals, some of the best of which also provided prayers suitable for public worship.

Another factor contributing to the great volume of material which has survived from the nineteenth century was the gradual adoption by the Free . Churches of written prayers in place of extempore. Two examples from Dr W. E. Orchard's Divine Service are included.

The early nineteenth century saw the beginning of the modern missionary movement, which found its ultimate fulfilment in the World Church of to-day. The prayer of Henry Martyn, a renowned pioneer of the movement, calls this to mind. A brilliant young scholar, he sailed to India in 1805 to preach the gospel of Christ and translate the New Testament into the languages of the people he served.

In Part IV we also have prayers from the great body of Victorian hymn-writers. Although hymns had been part of the Free Church tradition for a long time, the Church of England did not use hymns widely until the middle of the nineteenth century. The wider use of hymns can be dated from the publication in 1861 of Hymns Ancient and Modern – the brain-child of the Rev. Sir Henry Baker who wrote 'The King of Love my Shepherd is'. Hymn-writers have always provided prayers, and there are some typical examples in this part.

The setting for the final part, the twentieth century, saw Britain overshadowed by two world wars. This naturally brings about an emphasis in the prayers which reflects the needs and concerns of people facing the fears, uncertainties and realities of war. The prayers selected from those issued at different times cover a number of topics and are a clear call to the nation to pray. Although written in the actual war years, when the outcome was not known, they breathe a spirit of quiet confidence in God's unfailing mercy and power.

The new prayers from the Proposed Prayer Book of 1928 seem strangely old-fashioned now. At the time, the appearance of the book caused quite a stir in the Church and nation. It produced a major conflict between the Church Assembly, which approved it by a large majority, and the House of Commons which failed to give it assent.

Archbishop William Temple is remembered, among other things, for his great concern for social problems and also for Church unity. His prayers reflect these emphases and are marked by both dignity and sensitivity. Many other prayers in this part show the extent to which many of the scholarly leaders of the Church were able to combine a deep spirituality with a genuine and active concern for the daily lives of ordinary people and their needs.

Recent years have seen an immense number of new prayers by contemporary authors. To avoid making invidious choices, prayers by living authors have not in general been included.

In the final pages there are prayers from Ireland, Scotland and Wales which reflect something of the special concerns of these countries.

As the prayers follow an historical pattern, of necessity their subjects are mixed and often repetitive; but in their entirety they cover a wide variety of topics, as a glance in the Index of Subjects will show.

As is usual in an anthology of this kind, some of the prayers have been shortened and adapted; but as far as possible the original language of the prayers has been retained.

The prayers have been drawn from numerous sources and the task of collecting them has involved a certain amount of research. But, naturally, the standard collections now available have been of the greatest service, such as Dr Selina Fox's *Chain of Prayer Across the Ages*, dating back to 1913, Canon Macnutt's excellent *Prayer Manual*, and Dean Milner-White's *Daily Prayer*.

On a personal level I wish to express my thanks to Dr George Simms, formerly Archbishop of Armagh, for providing me with Irish prayers both old and new; and to the Rev. Derwyn Morris Jones, of the Union of Welsh Independents, and his colleague, the Rev. Rhys Nicholas, for several Welsh prayers supplied and translated.

Finally, I cannot fail to thank Mr Dick Douglas of Hodder & Stoughton, who initiated this project, for the help and encouragement he has given me in completing it.

Frank Colquhoun

PART I

THE EARLY CENTURIES TO THE END OF THE FIFTEENTH

Sectional prayers:

Prayers of the Celtic tradition

I
The Early Centuries

The breastplate of St Patrick

I RISE today with the power of God to guide me, the
might of God to uphold me, the wisdom of God
to teach me, the eye of God to watch over me, the
ear of God to hear me, the word of God to give me
speech, the hand of God to protect me, the path of
God to lie before me, the shield of God to shelter
me, the host of God to defend me against the snares
of the devil and the temptations of the world,
against every man who meditates injury to me,
whether far or near.

St Patrick, 373–461

CHRIST be with me, Christ before me, Christ
behind me,
Christ in me, Christ beneath me, Christ above me,
Christ on my right, Christ on my left,
Christ where I lie, Christ where I sit, Christ where
I arise,
Christ in the heart of every one who thinks of me,
Christ in the mouth of every one who speaks of
me,

Christ in every eye that sees me,
Christ in every ear that hears me.
  Salvation is of the Lord!
  May thy salvation, O Lord, be ever with us.

St Patrick

For perseverance

3 I PRAY my God to give me perseverance, and to vouchsafe that I bear to him faithful witness until my passing hence, for his Name's sake.

St Patrick, from 'The Confession'

For love and light

4 O LORD, give us we beseech thee in the Name of Jesus Christ thy Son our Lord, that love which can never cease, that will kindle our lamps but not extinguish them, that they may burn in us and enlighten others.

Do thou, O Christ, our dearest Saviour, thyself kindle our lamps that they may evermore shine in thy temple and receive unquenchable light from thee that will enlighten our darkness and lessen the darkness of the world.

St Columba of Iona, 521–97

The door of Paradise

ALMIGHTY God, Father, Son, and Holy Ghost, to   5
me the least of saints, to me allow that I may
keep a door in Paradise. That I may keep even the
small door, the farthest, darkest, coldest door, the
door that is least used, the stiffest door. If so it be in
thine house, O God, if so it be that I can see thy glory
even afar, and hear thy voice, and know that I am
with thee, O God.

St Columba

Invocation

MY dearest Lord,   6
be thou a bright flame before me,
be thou a guiding star above me,
be thou a smooth path beneath me,
be thou a kindly shepherd behind me,
today and for evermore.

St Columba

Song of creation

NOW must we praise the Lord,   7
The warden of heaven's realm,
The Creator's might and his mind's thought,
The glorious works of the Father:
How of every wonder he, the eternal Lord,
Laid the foundation;

How for the sons of men
He shaped heaven as their roof
And afterwards prepared the middle world,
The earth, for their habitation.

Caedmon, seventh century

Aspiration

8   OPEN our hearts, O Lord, and enlighten our minds by the grace of thy Holy Spirit, that we may seek what is well-pleasing to thy will; and so order our doings after thy commandments, that we may be found meet to enter into thine unending joys; through Jesus Christ our Lord.

The Venerable Bede, 673–735

9   I BESEECH thee, good Jesus, that as thou hast graciously granted to me here on earth sweetly to partake of the words of thy wisdom and knowledge, so thou wilt also vouchsafe that I may some time come to thee, the fountain of all wisdom, and always appear before thy face; who livest and reignest, world without end.

Bede

For protection

ALMIGHTY God, the only hope of the world, the only refuge for unhappy men, give me strong succour at this time and protect me from utter ruin, from facing the innumerable blows of the tyrant on my own. Remember I am dust and my life as fleeting as the flower of the field. May the eternal mercy that hath shone from time of old rescue thy servant from the jaws of the lion. Thou who didst come from on high in the cloak of flesh beat down the strongholds of the evil one, with thee the Captain of our salvation.

Bede

For our bishops

LORD Jesus Christ, who didst choose thine apostles that they might preside over us as teachers: may it also please thee to teach our bishops who serve in the place of thine apostles, and so to bless and instruct them that they may be preserved unharmed and undefiled in all their ways for evermore.

Egbert, d. 766, Archbishop of York

10

11

For our children

12 LOOK down from heaven, O Lord, upon the lambs of thy flock. Bless their bodies and their souls; and grant that they who have received thy sign, O Christ, on their foreheads may be thine own in the day of thine appearing; for thy Name's sake.

Egbert

The eternal God

13 ETERNAL Light, shine into our hearts,
Eternal Goodness, deliver us from evil,
Eternal Power, be our support,
Eternal Wisdom, scatter the darkness of our
    ignorance,
Eternal Pity, have mercy upon us;
    that with all our heart and mind and strength we
      may seek thy face and be brought by thine
      infinite mercy to thy holy presence; through
      Jesus Christ our Lord.

Alcuin of York, 735–804, priest and scholar

God's victorious servants

14 O KING of glory and Lord of valours, who hast said 'Be of good cheer, I have overcome the world': be thou victorious in us thy servants, for without thee we can do nothing. Grant thy compassion to go before us, thy compassion to come

behind us: before us in our undertakings, behind us in our ending. And what more shall we say but that thy will be done; for thy will is our salvation, our glory, and our joy.

Alcuin

Penitence

ALMIGHTY and merciful God, the fountain of all goodness, who knowest the thoughts of our hearts: we confess that we have sinned against thee, and done evil in thy sight. Wash us, we beseech thee, from the stains of our past sins, and give us grace and power to put away all hurtful things; that being delivered from the bondage of sin, we may bring forth fruits worthy of repentance, and at last enter into thy promised joy; through the mercy of thy blessed Son Jesus Christ our Lord. 15

Alcuin

Be thou my vision

BE thou my vision, beloved Lord; none other is aught 16
    but the King of the second heavens.
Be thou my meditation by day and night: may it be
    thee that I behold for ever in my sleep.

Be thou my speech, be thou my understanding: be
thou for me; may I be for thee.
Be thou my Father: may I be thy son; mayst thou
be mine: may I be thine.

Part of an eighth-century Irish poem, translated by Mary Byrne,
versified as a hymn by Eleanor Hull, 1912

The evil and the good

17 THREE things are of the evil one:
An evil eye,
An evil tongue,
An evil mind.
Three things are of God, and these three are what
Mary told her Son, for she heard them in heaven:
The merciful word,
The singing word,
And the good word.
May the power of these three holy things be on
all men and women of Erin for evermore.

Traditional Irish prayer

For strength and protection

18 LORD God Almighty, shaper and ruler of all thy
creatures, we pray thee of thy great mercy to
guide us to thy will and to the need of our souls,
better than we can ourselves.

Steadfast our minds towards thee; shield us against the temptations of the devil, and shield us from our foes, seen and unseen. Teach us, that we may inwardly love thee before all things, with a clean mind and a clean body.

For thou art our Maker and Redeemer, our help, our comforter, our hope and our trust. Praise and glory be to thee now and for evermore.

King Alfred, 849–c. 900

God's supremacy

To thee, O Lord our God we pray who art the supreme Truth;
    for all truth that is is from thee.
Thee we implore who art the highest Wisdom:
    all the wise are such through thee.
Thou art the supreme Joy:
    all who have become happy are so because of thee.
Thou art the highest Good:
    from thee all love and beauty spring.
Thou art the Light of the intellect:
    from thee man derives his understanding.

19

Adapted from King Alfred

Supplication

20   MAY the right hand of the Lord
keep us ever in old age,
the grace of our Lord Jesus Christ
continually defend us from the enemy.
O Lord, direct our hearts
in the way of peace.

Edelwald, ninth-century Saxon bishop

For spiritual understanding

21   ALMIGHTY God, who art the Essence of things
beyond space and time and yet within them:
manifest thyself unto us who feel after thee, seeking
thy light amid the shadows of ignorance. Recall us
from our errors and reach forth thy right hand to
help us, who without thee cannot come to thee and
who desire nothing beside thee; through Jesus
Christ our Lord.

John Scotus Erigena, ninth-century Irish scholar

Supplication for mercy

22   O LORD, O King, resplendent in the citadel of
heaven, whom all hail continually: of thy
clemency upon thy people do thou have mercy.

O Lord, whom the hosts of cherubim in songs
and hymns continually do praise: on us eternally
have mercy.

O Christ, enthroned as King above, whom the angels in their beauty praise without ceasing: deign thou upon us thy servants ever to have mercy.

O Christ, whom thy holy Church throughout the world doth magnify and adore: do thou have mercy upon us.

O Christ, whose holy ones, the heirs of the eternal country, one and all with utter joy proclaim in most worthy strains: do thou have mercy upon us.

O Lord, O gentle Son of Mary free, Blessed Redeemer, upon those who have been ransomed from the power of death by thine own blood, ever have mercy.

Derived from St Dunstan, 909–88, Archbishop of Canterbury

A birthday blessing

WE beseech thee, O Lord, open thy heavens; from thence may thy gifts descend to *him*. Put forth thine own hand and touch *his* head. May *he* feel the touch of thy hand, and receive the joy of the Holy Spirit, that *he* may remain blessed for evermore.

St Ethelwold, 908–84, Bishop of Winchester

The King's honour

24

MAY God of his goodness
and his great love,
keep me on my throne in honour
all my days.

Canute, 994–1035, King of England

Invocation of the Holy Spirit

25

HOLY Spirit of Love,
In us, around us, above,
Holy Spirit, we pray
Send sweet Jesus this day!

Holy Spirit to win
Body and soul within,
O Holy Spirit come!
Hallow our heart, thy home.

From the Irish of Maelishu O'Brolechain, 1086

Seeking God

26

LORD, I have sought thy face; thy face, Lord, will I
seek. Raise me up out of myself unto thee.
Cleanse, heal, quicken me; enlighten the eye of my
mind that it may look unto thee.

Grant that my soul may collect its strength once more and with all the power of my understanding strive after thee, O Lord.

Surely thou art life and wisdom, truth and blessedness, and everything that is truly good.

St Anselm, 1033–1109, Archbishop of Canterbury

In debt to God

I KNOW, O Lord, that because thou hast made me, to thee I owe myself; and that because thou hast redeemed me, to thee I owe more than myself. But more than myself I have not, and what I have I cannot give thee without myself. Do thou draw me unto thee, that being thine I may abide in thy likeness and in thy love for ever.

St Anselm

For the afflicted

WE bring before thee, O Lord, the troubles and perils of people and nations, the sighing of prisoners and captives, the sorrows of the bereaved, the necessities of strangers, the helplessness of the weak, the despondency of the weary, the failing powers of the aged. O Lord, draw near to each; for the sake of Jesus Christ our Lord.

St Anselm

Commendation

29 INTO thy hands, O Father and Lord, we commend our souls and bodies, our parents and homes, friends and servants, neighbours and kindred, our benefactors and brethren departed, all folk rightly believing, and all who need thy pity and protection. Light us all with thy holy grace, and suffer us never to be separated from thee, O Lord in Trinity, God everlasting.

St Edmund Rich, 1170–1240, Archbishop of Canterbury

Thanksgiving

30 THANKS be to thee, my Lord Jesus Christ,
　　For all the benefits thou hast won for me,
　For all the pains and insults thou hast borne for
　　me.
O most merciful Redeemer, Friend, and Brother,
　May I know thee more clearly,
　Love thee more dearly,
　And follow thee more nearly,
　　Now and for ever.

St Richard of Chichester, 1197–1253

God is my all

GOD, of thy goodness, give me thyself,   31
for thou art sufficient for me.
I may not ask for anything less
than what befits my full worship of thee.
If I were to ask anything less
I should always be in want,
for in thee alone do I have all.

The Lady Julian of Norwich, 1342–after 1413

Leaders of the nation

O GOD, Almighty Father, King of kings and   32
Lord of all our rulers, grant that the hearts and
minds of all who go out as leaders before us, the
statesmen, the judges, the men of learning, and the
men of wealth, may be so filled with the love of thy
laws, and of that which is righteous and life-giving,
that they may serve as a wholesome salt unto the
earth, and be worthy stewards of thy good and
perfect gifts; through Jesus Christ our Lord.

Prayer of the Order of the Garter, 1348

For pardon and purity

O HOLY God, whose mercy and pity made thee   33
descend from the high throne down into this
world for our salvation: mercifully forgive us all the
sins that we have done and thought and said. Send us

cleanness of heart and purity of soul; restore us with thy Holy Spirit, that we may henceforth live virtuously and love thee with all our hearts; through Jesus Christ thy Son.

Richard Rolle, 1349, English hermit

God's will

34 O LORD Jesus Christ, who hast made me and redeemed me and brought me where I am upon my way: thou knowest what thou wouldest do with me; do with me according to thy will, for thy tender mercies' sake.

King Henry VI, 1421–71

From forgetfulness

35 LORD of all mercy and goodness, suffer us not by any ingratitude or hardness of heart to forget the wonderful benefits that thou hast bestowed upon us this and every day; but grant that we may be mindful all the days of our life of the incomparable gifts which thou ever givest us through Jesus Christ our Lord.

Ancient Scottish prayer

The Creator

ALMIGHTY Creator, who hast made all things: 36
The world cannot express all thy glories,
Even though the grass and the trees should sing.
Thou hast wrought such a multitude of wonders
That they cannot be equalled or expressed.
It is not too great toil to praise the Trinity.
It is not too great toil to praise the Son of Mary.

Derived from an early Welsh poem

For protection

GUARD for me my eyes, Jesus Son of Mary,   37
lest seeing another's wealth make me
covetous.
Guard for me my ears, lest they harken to slander,
lest they listen to folly in the sinful world.
Guard for me my heart, O Christ, in thy love,
lest I ponder wretchedly the desire of any
iniquity.
Guard for me my hands, that they be not stretched
out for quarrelling or practise shameful
supplication.
Guard for me my feet upon the gentle earth of
Ireland, lest they be bent on profitless errands.

Early Irish

PRAYERS OF THE CELTIC TRADITION
of Scottish origin unless otherwise stated

Life's beginning and end

38

As thou wast before
At my life's beginning,
Be thou so again
    At my journey's end.

As thou wast besides
At my soul's shaping,
Father, be thou too
    At my journey's close.

The Trinity

39

THREE folds in my garment,
    yet only one garment I wear.
Three joints in my finger,
    yet only one finger is there.
Three leaves on a shamrock,
    yet only one shamrock I bear.
Three Persons in Godhead,
    yet only one God do I fear.

Irish

The homestead

GOD, bless the world and all that is therein;   40
God, bless my spouse and my children;
God, bless the eye that is within my head;
And, bless, O God, the handling of my hand.
God, protect the house and the household;
God, consecrate the children of the motherhood;
God, consecrate the flock and the young,
   What time the flocks ascend hill and wold,
   What time I lie down in peace to sleep.

For protection

DELIVER us, O God, from evil.   41
O Lord Jesus Christ, preserve us ever
   in all good works.
O fount and author of all good,
   replenish us with good virtues.
O God, empty us from faults,
   through thee, O Christ Jesu.

Peace

THOU commandest peace: 42
   thou givest peace.
Thou didst bequeath peace:
   Give us, O Lord, thy peace from heaven.
Make this day peaceful,
   and the remaining days of our life.

Supplication

43 THOU who guidedst Noah over the flood waves:
  Hear us.
Thou who with thy word recalled Jonah from the
  deep:
  Deliver us.
Thou who stretched forth thy hand to Peter as he
  sank:
  Help us, O Christ.
Son of God, who didst marvellous things of old:
  Be favourable in our day also.

Before or after prayer

44 ALMIGHTY Father, well-spring of life to all things
that have being, from amid the unwearied
praises of cherubim and seraphim who stand about
thy throne of light, give ear, we humbly beseech
thee, to the supplications of thy people who put
their sure trust in thy mercy; through Jesus Christ
our Lord.

For forgiveness

45 O GOD, who wouldest not the death of a sinner,
but that he should be converted and live: forgive the sins of us who turn to thee with all our
heart, and grant us the grace of eternal life, through
Jesus Christ our Lord.

The sunlight of heaven

I SEE the sunlight on the hills
    Of my Father's house,
Showing me the foundation
    Of my free salvation,
Showing me my name up there on the books of
        heaven,
And that nothing can ever blot it out.

Welsh

46

Our tongues

O JESUS, Son of God,
    Who wast silent before Pilate,
Do not let us wag our tongues
Without thinking of what we are to say
And of how to say it.

Irish

47

Joy

As the hand is made for holding and the eye for
seeing, thou hast fashioned me, O Lord, for
joy. Share with me the vision to find that joy
everywhere: in the wild violet's beauty, in the lark's
melody, in the face of a steadfast man, in a child's
smile, in a mother's love, in the purity of Jesus.

48

God guide me

49 G OD guide me with thy wisdom,
God chastise me with thy justice,
God help me with thy mercy,
God protect me with thy strength,
God shield me with thy shade,
God fill me with thy grace,
For the sake of thine anointed Son.

Praise

50 G LORIOUS Lord, I give you greeting!
Let the church and the chancel praise you,
Let the plain and the hillside praise you,
Let the dark and the daylight praise you,
Let the birds and the honeybees praise you,
Let the male and the female praise you,
And I shall praise you, Lord of glory:
Glorious Lord, I give you greeting!

Welsh

Benediction

51 B LESS to me, O God, the moon that is above me,
Bless to me, O God, the earth that is beneath
me,
Bless to me, O God, my wife and my children,
And bless, O God, myself who have the care of
them.

Harvest

THE seed is Christ's,
    The harvest is Christ's;   52
In the granary of God
May we be gathered.

The sea is Christ's,
The fishes are Christ's;
In the nets of God
May we all meet

Irish

My offering

I OFFER thee
  Every flower that ever grew,   53
Every bird that ever flew,
Every wind that ever blew,
                        Good God.

I offer thee
Every wave that ever moved,
Every heart that ever loved,
Thee, my Father's well-beloved,
                        Dear Lord.

I offer thee
Every flake of virgin snow,
Every spring of earth below,
Every human joy and woe,
                        My Love!

Irish

Peace be with you

54   DEEP peace of the running wave to you,
Deep peace of the flowing air to you,
Deep peace of the quiet earth to you,
Deep peace of the shining stars to you,
Deep peace of the Son of Peace to you,
for ever.

Things that are hateful to God

55   A WISE man without good words
An old man without religion
A young man without obedience
A rich man without alms
A woman without modesty
A master without virtue
A people without law.
Lord, pity me,
Lord, guard me.

Irish

PART II

THE REFORMATION
AND ELIZABETHAN
PERIOD

Sectional prayers:

Prayers of the Protestant Reformers
The Book of Common Prayer, 1549, 1552, 1559
General prayers of the Elizabethan era

2

The Reformation and Elizabethan Period

For forgiveness

O MOST merciful Father, who dost put away the sins of those who truly repent, we come before thy throne in the name of Jesus Christ, that for his sake alone thou wilt have compassion upon us, and let not our sins be a cloud between thee and us.

John Colet, 1467–1519, Dean of St Paul's

56

For God's gracious aid

G LORIOUS God, give me grace to amend my life, and to have an eye to mine end without grudge of death, which to them that die in thee, good Lord, is the fate of a wealthy life.

57

And give me, good Lord, an humble, lowly, quiet, peaceable, patient, charitable, kind, tender and pitiful mind, and with all my works, my words, and my thoughts to have a taste of thy holy, blessed Spirit.

Give me, good Lord, a full faith, a firm hope, and a fervent charity, a love to thee incomparable above the love to myself.

Give me, good Lord, a longing to be with thee,
not for the avoiding of the calamities of this world,
nor so much for the attaining of the joys of heaven,
as for a very love of thee.

Sir Thomas More, 1478–1535, written a few days before his execution

God within

58 G OD be in my head,
   and in my understanding;
God be in my eyes,
 and in my looking;
God be in my mouth,
 and in my speaking;
God be in my heart,
 and in my thinking;
God be at my end,
 and at my departing.

Book of Hours, 1514

The gift of faith

59 A LMIGHTY and everlasting God, who not only
givest every good and perfect gift, but also dost
increase those gifts that thou hast given: increase in
us the gift of faith, that we may truly believe in thee
and in thy promises made unto us; and that neither
by our negligence, nor infirmity of the flesh, nor
grievousness of temptation, we be driven from faith
in our Lord and Saviour Jesus Christ.

Anon. Household of King Henry VIII

For knowledge of God's word

GRANT unto us, O merciful God, knowledge and true understanding of thy word, that we may know what thy will is, and also may show forth in our lives those things that we do know; that we be not only knowers of thy word, but also doers of the same; by our Lord and Saviour Jesus Christ.

60

Anon, as above

For trust in God's providence

HOLD us fast, O Lord of Hosts, that we fall not from thee. Grant us thankful and obedient hearts, that we may increase daily in the love, knowledge and fear of thee. Increase our faith, and help our unbelief; that being provided for and relieved of all our needs by thy fatherly care and providence, we may live a godly life, to the praise and good example of thy people, and after this life may reign with thee for ever; through Jesus Christ our Saviour.

61

James Pilkington, 1520–76, Bishop of Durham

Commitment of life to Christ

62 O LORD Jesu, who art the only health of all men living, and the everlasting life of those who die in thy faith: I give myself wholly unto thy will, being sure that the thing cannot perish which is committed unto thy mercy.

Thomas Cromwell. Part of a prayer he repeated before his execution, July 1540

The jewel of God's word

63 O GRACIOUS God and most merciful Father, who hast vouchsafed to us the rich and precious jewel of thy holy word: assist us with thy Spirit that it may be written in our hearts to our everlasting comfort, to reform us, to renew us according to thine own image, to build us up in the perfect building of thy Christ, and to increase in us all heavenly virtues. Grant this, O heavenly Father, for the same Jesus Christ's sake.

From the Geneva Bible. Attributed to King Edward VI, 1537–53

Submission to God's will

64 O MERCIFUL God, be thou now unto us a strong tower of defence. Give us grace to await thy leisure, and patiently to bear what thou doest unto us, nothing doubting thy goodness towards us, for thou knowest what is good for us better than we do.

Therefore do for us in all things as thou wilt. Only arm us, we beseech thee, with thy armour, that we may stand fast, praying always that we may refer ourselves wholly to thy will. We are assuredly persuaded that all thou doest cannot but be well; and unto thee be all honour and glory, both now and ever.

Lady Jane Grey, born 1537, executed on Tower Hill 1554,
at the age of sixteen

PRAYERS OF THE PROTESTANT REFORMERS

Christ the true Light

O LORD, thou greatest and most true Light, whence the light of the day doth spring! O Light, which dost lighten every man that cometh into the world! O thou Wisdom of the eternal Father, lighten my mind, that I may see only those things that please thee, and may be blinded to all other things. Grant that I may walk in thy ways, and that nothing else may be light and pleasant. 65

John Bradford, 1510–55, martyr

For the municipal authority

A LMIGHTY God, whose is the eternal only power, and other men's power but borrowed of thee: we beseech thee for those who hold office in this 66 borough; that holding it first from thee, they may use it for the general good and to thine honour; through Jesus Christ our Lord.

Derived from words of William Tyndale,
1494–1536, Bible translator and martyr

A benediction

67 THE mighty God of Jacob be with you to supplant his enemies, and give you the favour of Joseph.

The wisdom and the spirit of Stephen be with your heart and with your mouth, and teach your lips what they shall say, and how to answer all things.

He is our God, if we despair in ourselves and trust in him; and his is the glory.

William Tyndale

For judges and magistrates

68 HEAVENLY Father, at whose hand the weak shall suffer no wrong nor the mighty escape just judgment: pour thy grace upon thy servants our judges and magistrates, that by their true, faithful and diligent execution of justice and equity to all men equally, thou mayest be glorified, the commonwealth daily promoted and increased, and we all live in peace and quietness, godliness and virtue; through Jesus Christ our Lord.

Thomas Cranmer, 1489–1556, Archbishop of Canterbury,
reformer and martyr

For the mind of Christ

O THOU who in almighty power wast weak, and
in perfect excellency wast lowly, grant unto
us the same mind. All that we have which is our own
is naught; if we have any good in us it is wholly thy
gift. O Saviour, since thou, the Lord of heaven and
earth, didst humble thyself, grant unto us true
humility, and make us like thyself; and then, of thine
infinite goodness, raise us to thine everlasting glory;
who livest and reignest with the Father and the Holy
Ghost for ever and ever.

Archbishop Cranmer

69

For true repentance

WE beseech thee, good Lord, that it may please
thee to give us true repentance; to forgive us all
our sins, negligences, and ignorances; and to endue
us with the grace of thy Holy Spirit, to amend our
lives according to thy holy word.

Archbishop Cranmer, from The Litany, 1544

70

Loyalty to conviction

HEAVENLY Father, the Father of all wisdom,
understanding, and true strength, we beseech
thee look mercifully upon thy servants, and send thy
Holy Spirit into their hearts; that when they must
join to fight in the field for the glory of thy name,
they may be defended with the strength of thy right

71

hand, and may manfully stand in the confession of thy faith, and continue in the same unto their lives' end.

Nicholas Ridley, 1500–55, Bishop of London, reformer and martyr

★　　★　　★

For faith

72　O LORD God, suffer us not to lean to our own wisdom, nor to believe as blind faith fancieth, nor to seek salvation where superstition dreameth, but let our faith be grounded only on thy word; and give us grace truly to believe in thee, and with all our heart to put our trust in thee, to look for all good things of thee, to call upon thy blessed Name in adversity, and with joyful voices and more merry hearts to praise and magnify it in prosperity.

Thomas Becon, 1512–67, reformer

For love of Christ

73　O LORD Jesus Christ, draw thou our hearts unto thee; join them together in inseparable love, that we may abide in thee and thou in us, and that the everlasting covenant between us may stand sure for ever. Let the fiery darts of thy love pierce through all our slothful members and inward powers, that we, being happily wounded, may so become whole and sound. Let us have no lover but thyself alone; let us seek no joy nor comfort except in thee.

*Miles Coverdale, 1488–1568, Bishop of Exeter, Bible scholar
and reformer*

For increase in knowledge

O GRACIOUS Father, grant unto us who through
thy Son have known thy Name, that in such
knowledge and light of the truth we may increase
more and more; and that the love wherewith thou
lovest thy dear Son may be and remain in us; and
that he, our head, may in us his members continue
to work, live, and bring forth fruit acceptable unto
thee.

Bishop Coverdale

74

That God may protect his cause

O LORD, most strong and mighty God, thou
destroyest the counsels of the ungodly, and
riddest this world of tyrants, so that no counsel or
force can resist thine eternal counsel and determination. We thy poor creatures and humble servants do
most earnestly desire thee, for the love that thou hast
to thy well-beloved Son, our Lord and Saviour Jesus
Christ, that thou wilt look upon thy cause, for it is
thine, O Lord; and bring to naught all those things
that are against thee and thy holy Word.

John Knox, 1513–72, Scottish reformer

75

For Christ's flock

76 O GOD of all power, who hast called from death the great pastor of the sheep, our Lord Jesus: comfort and defend the flock which he hath redeemed by the blood of the eternal testament. Increase the number of true preachers; lighten the hearts of the ignorant; relieve the pains of such as be afflicted, especially of those that suffer for the testimony of the truth; by the power of our Lord Jesus Christ.

John Knox

For increase of faith

77 O MOST merciful Father, we beseech thee, for thy mercy's sake, continue thy grace and favour towards us. Let not the sun of thy gospel ever go down out of our hearts; let thy truth abide and be established among us for ever. Help our unbelief, increase our faith, and give us hearts to consider the time of our visitation. Through faith clothe us with Christ, that he may live in us, and thy Name may be glorified through us in all the world.

John Jewell, 1522–71, Bishop of Salisbury, reformer

Glorifying God

THE God and Father of our Lord Jesus Christ open   78
all our eyes, that we may see that blessed hope
to which we are called; that we may altogether
glorify the only true God and Jesus Christ, whom he
hath sent down to us from heaven; to whom with
the Father and the Holy Spirit be rendered all
honour and glory to all eternity.

Bishop Jewell

THE BOOK OF COMMON PRAYER
*Prayers from the versions of 1549 and 1552
(Edward VI) and 1559 (Elizabeth I)*

In times of trouble

WE humbly beseech thee, O Father, mercifully   79
to look upon our infirmities; and for the glory
of thy Name turn from us all those evils that we
most righteously have deserved; and grant that in all
our troubles we may put our whole trust and confidence in thy mercy, and evermore serve thee in
holiness and pureness of living, to thy honour and
glory; through our only Mediator and Advocate,
Jesus Christ our Lord.

The Litany, 1549

For peace

80   O GOD, who art the author of peace and lover of concord, in knowledge of whom standeth our eternal life, whose service is perfect freedom: defend us thy humble servants in all assaults of our enemies; that we, surely trusting in thy defence, may not fear the power of any adversaries; through the might of Jesus Christ our Lord.

Morning Prayer, 1549

The holy Scriptures

81   BLESSED Lord, who hast caused all holy Scriptures to be written for our learning: grant that we may in such wise hear them, read, mark, learn, and inwardly digest them, that by patience and comfort of thy holy Word, we may embrace and ever hold fast the blessed hope of everlasting life, which thou hast given us in our Saviour Jesus Christ.

Collect Advent II, 1549

Christmas

82   O GOD, who makest us glad with the yearly remembrance of the birth of thine only Son Jesus Christ: grant that as we joyfully receive him for our Redeemer, so we may with sure confidence behold him when he shall come to be our judge; who liveth and reigneth with thee and the Holy Ghost world without end.

First collect of Christmas, 1549

All Saints

O ALMIGHTY God, who hast knit together thine elect in one communion and fellowship, in the mystical body of thy Son Jesus Christ our Lord: grant us grace so to follow thy blessed saints in all virtuous and godly living, that we may come to those unspeakable joys, which thou hast prepared for them that unfeignedly love thee; through Jesus Christ our Lord.

83

Collect of All Saints' Day, 1549

The departed

A LMIGHTY God, with whom do live the spirits of them that depart hence in the Lord, and with whom the souls of the faithful, after they are delivered from the burden of the flesh, are in joy and felicity: we give thee hearty thanks, for that it hath pleased thee to deliver this our *brother* out of the miseries of this sinful world; beseeching thee that it may please thee, of thy gracious goodness, shortly to accomplish the number of thine elect, and to hasten thy kingdom; that we, with all those that are departed in the true faith of thy holy Name, may have our perfect consummation and bliss, both in body and soul, in thy eternal and everlasting glory; through Jesus Christ our Lord.

84

The Burial of the Dead, 1549

After divine service

85 ALMIGHTY God, who hast promised to hear the petitions of them that ask in thy Son's Name: we beseech thee mercifully to incline thine ears to us that have now made our prayers and supplications unto thee; and grant that those things, which we have faithfully asked according to thy will, may effectually be obtained, to the relief of our necessity, and to the setting forth of thy glory; through Jesus Christ our Lord.

Post Communion collect, 1549

The Blessing

86 THE peace of God, which passeth all understanding, keep your hearts and minds in the knowledge and love of God, and of his Son Jesus Christ our Lord: and the blessing of God Almighty, the Father, the Son, and the Holy Ghost, be amongst you and remain with you always.

Holy Communion, 1549

A general confession

87 ALMIGHTY and most merciful Father, we have erred and strayed from thy ways like lost sheep, we have followed too much the devices and desires of our own hearts, we have offended against thy holy laws. We have left undone those things which we ought to have done, and we have done those

things which we ought not to have done, and there is no health in us. But thou, O Lord, have mercy upon us miserable offenders; spare thou them, O God, which confess their faults; restore thou them that are penitent, according to thy promises declared unto mankind in Christ Jesus our Lord. And grant, O most merciful Father, for his sake, that we may hereafter live a godly, righteous, and sober life, to the glory of thy holy Name.

Morning and Evening Prayer, 1552

In the time of war and tumults

O ALMIGHTY God, King of all kings, and Governor of all things, whose power no creature is able to resist, to whom it belongeth justly to punish sinners, and to be merciful to them that truly repent: save and deliver us, we humbly beseech thee, from the hands of our enemies; abate their pride, assuage their malice, and confound their devices; that we, being armed with thy defence, may be preserved evermore from all perils, to glorify thee, who art the only giver of all victory; through the merits of thy only Son, Jesus Christ our Lord.

Occasional Prayers, 1552

Saint Andrew

89 A LMIGHTY God, who didst give such grace unto thy holy Apostle Saint Andrew, that he readily obeyed the calling of thy Son Jesus Christ, and followed him without delay: grant us all, that we, being called by thy holy Word, may forthwith give up ourselves obediently to fulfil thy holy commandments; through the same Jesus Christ our Lord.

Collect of St Andrew's Day, 1552

For increase in the Holy Spirit

90 D EFEND, O Lord, this thy child [or *this thy servant*] with thy heavenly grace, that *he* may continue thine for ever; and daily increase in thy Holy Spirit, more and more, until *he* come unto thy everlasting kingdom.

Order of Confirmation, 1552

For the Queen's Majesty

91 O LORD our heavenly Father, high and mighty, King of kings, Lord of lords, the only ruler of princes, who dost from thy throne behold all the dwellers upon earth: most heartily we beseech thee with thy favour to behold our most gracious Sovereign Lady, Queen Elizabeth; and so replenish her with the grace of thy Holy Spirit, that she may alway incline to thy will, and walk in thy way.

Endue her plenteously with heavenly gifts; grant her in health and wealth long to live; strengthen her that she may vanquish and overcome all her enemies, and finally, after this life, she may attain everlasting joy and felicity; through Jesus Christ our Lord.

Morning and Evening Prayer, 1559

A prayer for clergy and people

ALMIGHTY and everlasting God, who alone workest great marvels: send down upon our Bishops and Curates, and all congregations committed to their charge, the healthful Spirit of thy grace; and that they may truly please thee, pour upon them the continual dew of thy blessing. Grant this, O Lord, for the honour of our Advocate and Mediator, Jesus Christ.

92

Morning and Evening Prayer, 1559

After prayer

O GOD, whose nature is ever to have mercy and to forgive, receive our humble petitions; and though we be tied and bound with the chain of our sins, yet let the pitifulness of thy great mercy loose us; for the honour of Jesus Christ, our Mediator and Advocate.

93

Occasional Prayers, 1559

At the end of worship

94 THE grace of our Lord Jesus Christ, and the love of God, and the fellowship of the Holy Ghost, be with us all evermore.

Morning and Evening Prayer, 1559

★　　★　　★

Lord, set me free

95 O LORD my God, I have hope in thee;
O my dear Jesus, set me free.
Though hard the chains that fasten me
And sore my lot, yet I long for thee.
I languish and groaning bend my knee,
Adoring, imploring, O set me free.

Mary Queen of Scots, 1542–87, on the eve of her execution

For the nation

96 O LORD God everlasting, who reigneth over the kingdoms of men, so teach me thy Word and so strengthen me with thy grace that I may feed thy people with a faithful and true heart, and rule them prudently with power.

I acknowledge, O my King, that without thee my throne is unstable, my seat unsure, my kingdom tottering, my life uncertain. I see all things in this life subject to mutability.

Therefore, O Lord, create in me a new heart, and so renew my spirit that thy law may be my study, thy truth my delight, thy Church my care, thy people my crown, thy righteousness my pleasure, thy service my government.

So shall this my kingdom through thee be established with peace.

From a private prayer of Queen Elizabeth, 1533–1603

For the fleet

O LORD, thine enemies know that thou hast received England into thine own protection. Set a wall about it, O Lord, and evermore mightily defend it.

Let it be a comfort to the afflicted, a help to the oppressed, and a defence to thy Church and people persecuted abroad.

And forasmuch as this cause is now in hand, direct and go before our armies, both by sea and land. Bless them and prosper them, and grant unto them honourable success and victory.

Written by Queen Elizabeth for use in churches before the fleet sailed, 1588

97

For good success

98 GIVE ear, O God, to the prayers of thy people, that our service may take such good effect as thou mayest be glorified, thy Church, our Sovereign and country preserved, and every enemy of the truth so utterly vanquished that we may have continual peace; through Jesus Christ our Lord.

After Sir Francis Drake, 1540–96

Commitment

99 WHAT shall befall us hereafter we know not; but to God, who cares for all men, we commit ourselves wholly, with all who are near and dear to us.

And we beseech the same Almighty and most merciful God that for the time to come we may so bear the reproach of Christ with unbroken courage, as ever to remember that here we have no continuing city, but may seek one to come by the grace and mercy of our Lord Jesus Christ; to whom with the Father and the Holy Ghost be all honour and dominion, world without end.

Matthew Parker, 1504–75, Archbishop of Canterbury

Praise and thanksgiving

GLORY be to God in the highest, the creator and 100
Lord of heaven and earth, the preserver of all
things, the Father of mercies, who so loved mankind as to send his only begotten Son into the world,
to redeem us from sin and misery, and to obtain for
us everlasting life.

Accept, O gracious God, our praises and thanksgiving for thine infinite mercies towards us; and
teach us, O Lord, to love thee more and serve thee
better; through Jesus Christ our Lord.

John Hamilton, 1511–71, Archbishop of St Andrews

For heavenly-mindedness

TAKE from us, O God, the care of earthly vanities; 101
make us content with necessities. Keep our
hearts from delighting in honours, treasures, and
pleasures of this life, and engender in us a desire to be
with thee in thy eternal kingdom. And give us such
taste and feeling for thy unspeakable joys in heaven
that we may always long for them, and with all thy
people pray for the hastening of thy kingdom; for
the sake of Jesus Christ our Lord.

Edmund Grindal, 1519–83, Archbishop of Canterbury

Easter

102

Most glorious Lord of Life, that on this day
Didst make thy triumph over death and sin;
And, having harrowed hell, didst bring away
Captivity thence captive, us to win:
This joyous day, dear Lord, with joy begin;
And grant that we, for whom thou didst die,
Being with thy dear blood clean washed from sin,
May live for ever in felicity.
And that thy love, we weighing worthily,
May likewise love thee for the same again;
And for thy sake, that all like dear didst buy,
With love may one another entertain.
So let us love, dear Love, like as we ought.
Love is the lesson which the Lord us taught.

Edmund Spenser, 1552–99

A Child my Choice

103

Let folly praise that fancy loves, I praise and love
the Child
Whose heart no thought, whose tongue no word,
whose hand no deed defiled.
I praise him most, I love him best, all praise and
love is his;
While him I love, in him I live, and cannot live
amiss.

Love's sweetest mark, laud's highest theme,
man's most desirèd light,
To love him life, to leave him death, to live in him
delight.

He mine by gift, I his by debt, thus each to other
    due.
First friend he was, best friend he is, all times will
    try him true . . .

Almighty Babe, whose tender arms can force all
    foes to fly,
Correct my faults, protect my life, direct me when
    I die!

Robert Southwell, 1561–95, Jesuit martyr

GENERAL PRAYERS OF THE ELIZABETHAN ERA

Following Christ

O SAVIOUR Christ, who dost lead to eternal blessedness those who commit themselves to thee: grant that we, being weak, may not presume to trust in ourselves, but may always have thee before our eyes to follow as our guide; that thou, who alone knowest the way, may lead us to our heavenly desires. To thee with the Father and the Holy Ghost be glory for ever.

104

Primer of 1545

God our refuge and strength

105   ALMIGHTY God, let thy comfort support and strengthen us; and then receive unto thyself, O Father, that which thy power hath shapen; receive, O Lord the Son, that which thou hast bought us, with thy precious blood; receive, O Lord the Holy Ghost, that which thou hast kept and preserved so lovingly in this evil world.

And to thee, who art over all, three persons and one God, be praise and honour for ever and ever.

Primer of 1545

The Church in our land

106   CONTINUE, O Lord, thy most holy word and gospel in this realm of England, and grant that we may truly and thankfully embrace it. Give peace to thy Church from external troubles and persecutions, and from domestic discord and dissension; that all who profess thy word and gospel may have the same as well in heart as in mouth; for our Lord Jesus Christ's sake.

Undated, pre-Elizabethan

For perseverance in faith

107   O MERCIFUL Lord God, heavenly Father, we heartily beseech thee that thou wilt vouchsafe to take care and charge of us. Suffer us not to perish

in the works of darkness, but to kindle the light of thy truth in our hearts; that thy godly knowledge may daily increase in us through a right and pure faith, and that we may always be found to walk and live after thy will and pleasure.

Primer of 1553

Commemoration of the departed

ALMIGHTY God, we offer unto thee most high praise and hearty thanks for the wonderful graces and virtues which thou hast manifested in all thy saints and in all other holy persons upon earth, who by their lives and labours have shined forth as lights in the world, whom we remember with honour and commemorate with joy. For these and for all thy other servants who have departed this life with the seal of faith, we praise and magnify thy holy Name; through Jesus Christ our Lord.

108

Scottish Liturgy, 1560

A morning prayer

ALMIGHTY and most gracious God, we heartily thank thee for the sleep and rest which thou hast given us this night past; and forasmuch as thou hast commanded by thy holy word that no man should be idle, but all given continually to every good work, every man according to his calling, we most humbly beseech thee that thy love may daily attend

109

upon us, defend, nourish, comfort, and govern us and all our labours; and grant that we may spend this day according to thy most holy will; through Jesus Christ our Lord.

Christian Prayers, 1566

An evening prayer

110 O LORD Jesus Christ, our watchman and keeper, take us into thy care, and grant that, our bodies sleeping, our minds may watch in thee and be made merry by some sight of that celestial and heavenly life wherein thou art the King and Prince, together with the Father and the Holy Ghost, where thy angels and holy souls be most happy citizens. O purify our souls, keep clean our bodies, that in both we may please thee, sleeping and waking, for ever.

Christian Prayers, 1566

Love of God

111 O GOD, who doth infuse the gifts of charity into the hearts of the faithful through the grace of thy Holy Ghost: grant unto thy servants, both men and women for whom we pray unto thy mercy, health of body and soul, that they may love thee with all their power, and perform with all love the things that may be pleasing to thee; through Jesus Christ our Lord.

Primer of 1557

God's bountiful gifts

THE eyes of all do look up and trust in thee, O   112
Lord. Thou givest them their meat in due
season, thou dost open thy hand and fillest with thy
blessing everything living. Good Lord, bless us and
all thy gifts which we receive of thy bountiful
liberality; through Jesus Christ our Lord.

Queen Elizabeth's Primer, 1558

The light of Christ

O LORD Jesus Christ, who art the very bright sun   113
of the world, ever rising and never going
down: shine, we beseech thee, upon our spirit, that
the night of sin and error being driven away by thy
inward light, we may walk without stumbling, as in
the day. Grant this, O Lord, who livest and reignest
with the Father and the Holy Ghost for evermore.

Primer of 1559

For concord in the Church

IN thy household the Church, O Lord, let us dwell   114
in peace and concord. Give us all one heart, one
mind, one true interpretation of thy word; that all
who believe in thee may together extol thy Name,
O Lord God, most glorious and excellent over all.

From Godly Prayers, 1559

The witness of the Spirit

115 ALMIGHTY and merciful Lord, who givest unto thy faithful people the Holy Ghost, as a sure pledge of thy heavenly kingdom: grant unto us this Holy Spirit, that he may bear witness with our spirit that we be thy children and heirs of thy kingdom; by our Lord Jesus Christ.

Godly Prayers, 1559

Invocation

116 GOD grant to the living, grace; to the departed, rest; to the Church, the Queen, the Commonwealth, and to all mankind, peace and concord; and to us and all his servants, life everlasting.

Elizabethan

Against carefulness

117 O LORD, take from me a careful heart in all worldly things, and grant that neither poverty oppress me and drive me to despair or falsehood, nor prosperity lift me up to forget thee or myself; but that in prosperity I may be thankful, and in adversity patient and humble. Make me merry without lightness, sad without mistrust, sober without dullness, fearing thee without desperation, trusting in thee without presumption.

Henry Bull, Christian Prayers, 1578

The malicious tempter

O LORD God who knowest that, whiles we go a
warfare in these tents of our bodies, the ma-
licious tempter, from whose tyranny thou hast set
us free by thy Son Jesus Christ, ceaseth not to try all
his policies to draw us back again into bondage; we
beseech thee, give us not over into his hands for
want of defence, but grant us such grace that we,
continuing in the fellowship of thy most loving Son
through faith and charity, may finally come to the
life where there is no stumbling, nor any danger
more through fear of the enemy.

Christian Prayers, 1578

118

The Church universal

B E merciful, O Father of all mercies, to thy
Church universal dispersed throughout the
whole world; and grant that all that confess thy holy
Name may agree in the truth of thy holy word, and
live in godly concord and unity. And especially be
merciful to such as are under persecution for the
testimony of their conscience, and for the profession
of the gospel of thy Son, our Saviour Jesus Christ.

Prayers of 1585

119

The House of Commons

120

ALMIGHTY God, by whom alone kings reign and princes decree justice, and from whom alone cometh all wisdom and understanding: we thine unworthy servants, here gathered together in thy Name, do most humbly beseech thee to send down thy heavenly wisdom from above, to direct and guide us in all our consultations; and grant that, we having thy fear always before our eyes, and laying aside all private interests, prejudices, and partial affections, the result of all our counsels may be the glory of thy blessed Name, the maintenance of true religion and justice, the safety, honour, and happiness of the Sovereign, the public welfare, peace and tranquillity of the realm, and the uniting and knitting together of the hearts of all persons and estates within the same in true Christian love and charity towards one another; through Jesus Christ our Lord and Saviour.

Prayer used at every sitting of the House, composed by Sir Christopher Yelverton, MP for Northampton, about 1578

Praise

121

MOST worthy art thou, O good and gracious God, of all praise, even for thine own sake which exceedeth all things in holiness. By thee only are we hallowed and made holy. As our duty continually bids us, we praise thee for our glorious redemption, purchased for us in thy dearly beloved Son Jesus Christ. And grant that all things that breathe with life may praise thee; through the same Jesus Christ our Lord, who reigneth with thee and the Holy Ghost, one God, for ever and ever.

The Iona Books, 1595

A new song

INSTRUCT our mouths, O good Lord, with a new song, that our hearts being renewed, we may sing in the company of thy saints and rejoice in thee our Creator and Redeemer. Grant us such peace of conscience that may strengthen our work in thee, and being girt with the two-edged sword of thy word and Holy Spirit we may strive against all things that oppose themselves to the glory of thy most holy Name; through Jesus Christ thy dear Son, our only Lord and Redeemer.

122

Scottish Psalter, 1595

For all nations

ALMIGHTY and everlasting God, who hast wrought the redemption of mankind after a miraculous manner, in sending thy only Son to fulfil the promises made to our fathers; open up more and more the knowledge of that salvation, that in all places of the earth thy truth and power may be made known, to the intent that all nations may praise, honour, and glorify thy selfsame Son Jesus Christ.

123

Scottish Psalter, 1595

73

The God of peace

124   GRACIOUS Lord, thou art not the God of confusion or discord but the God of peace and
concord; unite our hearts and affections in such sort
together, that we may walk in thy house in brotherly love and as members of the body of Christ. Let
the oil of sanctification that is thy Holy Spirit in-
flame us, and the dew of thy blessing continually fall
upon us; that we may obtain life eternal through the
same Jesus thy Son.

Scottish Psalter, 1595

The nations' mutual service

125   ALMIGHTY God, Maker of all things, who hast
placed they creatures necessary for the use of
man in diverse lands: grant that all men and nations,
needing one another, may be knit together in one
bond of mutual service, to share their diverse riches;
through Jesus Christ our Lord.

Sixteenth-century, adapted

PART III

THE SEVENTEENTH
AND
EIGHTEENTH
CENTURIES

Sectional Prayers:

Prayers of Bishop Lancelot Andrewes
The Book of Common Prayer, 1662
Prayers of Bishop Jeremy Taylor
Prayers of famous men and women of the period
Prayers of the poets of the period

3

The Seventeenth and Eighteenth Centuries

A bidding prayer

L ET us pray for Christ's Holy Catholic Church, 126
that is, for the whole congregation of Christian
people dispersed throughout the whole world,
and for all ministers of God's holy Word and
Sacraments.

For our Sovereign Lady, Queen Elizabeth, and
those in authority under her, that all and every one
of them, in their several callings, may serve truly to
the glory of God and the edifying and well-
governing of her people, remembering the solemn
account which they must make.

Pray we also for all people of this realm, that
they may live in the true faith and fear of God, in
obedience to our laws, and in brotherly charity to
one another.

Finally, let us praise God for all those who are
departed out of this life in the faith of Christ, and
pray unto God that we may have grace to direct our
lives after their good examples; that this life ended,
we may be made partakers with them of the glorious
resurrection in the life everlasting.

From the Canons of 1603

A soldier's prayer

127 ARM me, O thou God of battles, with courage this day, that I may not fall before my enemies. The quarrel is thine, let the victory be thine. Tie to my sinews the strength of David that may with a pebble-stone strike to the earth these giants that fight against thy truth . . . So let me fight that, whether I come off lame or sound, dead or alive, I may live or die thy soldier.

Thomas Dekker, 1609

Preparation for worship

128 O GOD, we humbly beseech thee to purify our hearts from all vain, worldly and sinful thoughts, and so prepare our souls to worship thee this day acceptably, with reverence and godly fear.

Set our affections on things above all the day long, and give us grace to receive thy Word which we shall hear into honest and good hearts, and bring forth fruit with patience; for the sake of Jesus Christ our Saviour.

Gavin Hamilton, 1561–1612, Bishop of Galloway

For those in authority

129 BLESS, O Lord, those whom thou hast set over us, both in Church and State. Govern their hearts in thy fear, and guide their understanding to do those

things which are acceptable to thee; that they may faithfully serve thy people, and set forward thy everlasting kingdom; through Jesus Christ our Lord.

Bishop Hamilton

For those we love

WE call to mind, O God, before thy throne of grace all those whom thou hast given to be near and dear to us, and all for whom we are specially bound to pray; beseeching thee to remember them all for good, and to fulfil as may be expedient for them all their desires and wants. We commend to thee any who may have wronged us, by word or deed, beseeching thee to forgive them and us all our sins, and to bring us to thy heavenly kingdom; through Jesus Christ our Lord.

Bishop Hamilton

For guidance and strength

O THOU great God of life and death, eternal Maker and Mover, whose will is the first of causes, and whose glory is the last of ends: direct our feet to the place which thou hast appointed; strengthen then these poor hands to accomplish thy pleasure, and let heaven and earth obey thee.

Sir Henry Wotton, 1568–1639

PRAYERS OF BISHOP LANCELOT ANDREWES, 1555–1626

For the nation

132   O KING of the nations unto the ends of the earth, strengthen all the commonwealths of the world as thine institution, albeit the ordinance of man.

Scatter, O Lord, the peoples that make for war; and deliver this island, and the countries wherein we sojourn, from all tribulation, peril and necessity.

Remember our Queen, and give her prosperity in all things.

Grant unto them that are eminent in station to be eminent for virtue and for fear of thee; to the Parliament thy holy prudence; to our powerful men to have no power against the truth, but for the truth.

Grant to our people to be subject unto rule not only for wrath but also for conscience's sake; and thy peace and love bestow upon us all, O Lord our God.

For the Church

133   O LORD, we pray for the Universal Church, for all sections of thy Church throughout the world, for their truth, unity, and stability, that love may abound, and truth flourish in them all.

We pray for our own Church, that what is lacking in it may be supplied, and what is unsound corrected; and unto all men everywhere give thy grace and thy blessing; for the sake of Jesus Christ, our only Lord and Saviour.

For the departed

REMEMBER, O Lord, thy servants and hand-maidens who have departed hence in thy Name, especially . . . and all others to whom our remembrance is due. Give them eternal rest and peace, and to us such a measure of communion with them as thou knowest to be best for us. And bring us all to serve thee in thine eternal kingdom, when thou wilt and as thou wilt, only without shame or sin; through Jesus Christ our Lord.

134

For grace

O GOD our Father, let us find grace in thy sight so as to have grace to serve thee acceptably with reverence and godly fear. And further grace not to receive thy grace in vain, nor to neglect it and fall from it, but to stir it up and grow in it, and to persevere in it unto the end of our lives; through Jesus Christ our Lord.

135

Commendation

136

WE commend unto thee, O Lord,
    our souls and our bodies,
our minds and our thoughts,
our prayers and our hopes,
our health and our work,
our life and our death;
our parents and brothers and sisters,
    our benefactors and friends,
      our neighbours, our countrymen,
      and all Christian folk,
        this day and always.

Doxology

137

BLESSING and honour, thanksgiving and praise,
    more than we can utter,
more than we can conceive,
be unto thee, O holy and glorious Trinity,
    Father, Son, and Holy Spirit,
by all angels, all men, all creatures,
    for ever and ever.

NOTE *Lancelot Andrewes, Bishop first of Chichester, then of Winchester, was a devoted scholar and one of the translators of the Authorised Version of the Bible.*

★   ★   ★

Heaven

138

BRING us, O Lord our God, at our last awakening into the house and gate of heaven, to enter into that gate and dwell in that house, where there shall be no darkness nor dazzling, but one equal light; no noise nor silence, but one equal music; no fears nor hopes, but one equal possession; no ends nor beginnings, but one equal eternity; in the habitations of thy glory and dominion world without end.

John Donne, 1572–1631, Dean of St Paul's

For consistent Christian living

LORD, thou hast made thyself to be ours, therefore now show thyself to us in thy wisdom, goodness, and power.   139

To walk faithfully in our Christian course we need much grace: supply us out of thy rich store.

We need wisdom to go in and out inoffensively before others: furnish us with thy Spirit.

We need patience and comfort: thou that art the God of consolation bestow it upon us; for Christ's sake.

Richard Sibbes, 1577–1635, Puritan divine

For the nation

LORD, bless this Kingdom, we beseech thee, that religion and virtue may season all sorts of men;   140
that there may be peace within its gates and prosperity in all its borders. In peace so preserve it that it corrupt not; in trouble so defend it that it suffer not;

and so order it, whether in plenty or in want, that it may patiently and peaceably seek thee, the only full supply and sure foundation of both men and states; that so it may continue a place and people to do thee service to the end of time; through Jesus Christ our only Saviour and Redeemer.

William Laud, 1573–1645, Archbishop of Canterbury

For the Church

141   MOST gracious Father, we most humbly beseech thee for thy Holy Catholic Church. Fill it with all truth; in all truth with all peace. Where it is corrupt, purge it; where it is in error, direct it; where anything is amiss, reform it; where it is right, strengthen and confirm it; where it is in want, furnish it; where it is divided and rent asunder, make up the breaches of it, O thou Holy One of Israel.

Archbishop Laud

For ourselves

142   GRANT, O Lord, that we may
     live in thy fear,
die in thy favour,
rest in thy peace,

> rise in thy power,
> reign in thy glory;
> for thine own beloved Son's sake,
> Jesus Christ our Lord.

Archbishop Laud

Christ the King

O ALMIGHTY God, vouchsafe so to reign in our souls that Christ may have the sole dominion there; that we may sincerely embrace him with our whole hearts, honour him with all our faculties, confess him with our tongues, and glorify him by our works, together with thee, O Father, and the blessed Spirit, now and for ever.

George Wither, 1588–1667

143

The holy war

O GOD, the Lord and leader of the hosts of the blessed, instruct us in the spiritual warfare. Arm us against all foes visible and invisible; subdue unto us our own rebellious affections; and give us daily victory in the following of him who vanquished sin and death, and now goeth forth with us conquering and to conquer, even thy Son our Saviour Jesus Christ.

George Wither

144

THE BOOK OF COMMON PRAYER
Prayers added in the version of 1662

For the High Court of Parliament

145 Most gracious God, we humbly beseech thee, as for this Kingdom in general, so especially for the High Court of Parliament, under our most religious and gracious Queen at this time assembled; that thou wouldest be pleased to direct and prosper all their consultations to the advancement of thy glory, the good of thy Church, the safety, honour, and welfare of our Sovereign and her Dominions; that all things may be so ordered and settled by their endeavours, upon the best and surest foundations, that peace and happiness, truth and justice, religion and piety, may be established among us for all generations. These and all other necessaries, for them, for us, and thy whole Church, we humbly beg in the name and mediation of Jesus Christ our most blessed Lord and Saviour.

Archbishop Laud, Occasional Prayers

For all conditions of men

146 O GOD, the Creator and Preserver of all mankind, we humbly beseech thee for all sorts and conditions of men; that thou wouldest be pleased to make thy ways known unto them, thy saving health unto all nations. More especially we pray for the good estate of the Catholick Church; that it may be so guided and governed by thy good Spirit, that all

who profess and call themselves Christians may be led into the way of truth, and hold the faith in unity of spirit, in the bond of peace, and in righteousness of life.

Finally we commend to thy fatherly goodness all those who are any ways afflicted or distressed in mind, body, or estate; that it may please thee to comfort and relieve them, according to their several necessities, giving them patience under their sufferings, and a happy issue out of all their afflictions. And this we beg for Jesus Christ his sake.

Peter Gunning, Bishop of Ely, Occasional Prayers

A general thanksgiving

ALMIGHTY God, Father of all mercies, we thine unworthy servants do give thee most humble and hearty thanks for all thy goodness and loving-kindness to us and to all men. We bless thee for our creation, preservation, and all the blessings of this life; but above all for thine inestimable love in the redemption of the world by our Lord Jesus Christ, for the means of grace, and for the hope of glory.

147

And we beseech thee, give us that due sense of all thy mercies, that our hearts may be unfeignedly thankful, and that we show forth thy praise, not only with our lips, but in our lives; by giving up ourselves to thy service, and by walking before thee in holiness and righteousness all our days; through

Jesus Christ our Lord, to whom with thee and the Holy Ghost be all honour and glory, world without end.

Edward Reynolds, Bishop of Norwich, Thanksgivings

For ministers of the gospel

148 O LORD Jesus Christ, who at thy first coming didst send thy messenger to prepare thy way before thee: grant that the ministers and stewards of thy mysteries may likewise so prepare and make ready thy way, by turning the hearts of the disobedient to the wisdom of the just, that at thy second coming to judge the world we may be found an acceptable people in thy sight; who livest and reignest with the Father and the Holy Spirit, ever one God, world without end.

John Cosin, Bishop of Durham, Collect of the Third Sunday in Advent

For ordinands

149 A LMIGHTY God, giver of all good gifts, who of thy divine providence hast appointed diverse Orders in thy Church: give thy grace, we humbly beseech thee, to all those who are to be called to any office and administration in the same; and so replenish them with the truth of thy doctrine, and endue them with innocency of life, that they may faithfully

serve before thee, to the glory of thy great Name,
and the benefit of thy holy Church; through Jesus
Christ our Lord.

Embertide Collect

Veni, Creator Spiritus

COME, Holy Ghost, our souls inspire,   150
And lighten with celestial fire.
Thou the anointing Spirit art,
Who dost thy sevenfold gifts impart.

Thy blessed Unction from above
Is comfort, life, and fire of love.
Enable with perpetual light
The dullness of our blinded sight.

Anoint and cheer our soilèd face
With the abundance of thy grace.
Keep far our foes, give peace at home,
Where thou art guide, no ill can come.

Teach us to know the Father, Son,
And thee, of both, to be but One.
That, through the ages all along,
This may be our endless song:
    Praise to thy eternal merit,
    Father, Son, and Holy Spirit.

Translated by Bishop Cosin, The Ordinal

Prayer of the Royal Navy

151 O ETERNAL Lord God, who alone spreadest out the heavens, and rulest the raging of the sea; who hast compassed the waters with bounds until day and night come to an end: be pleased to receive into thy Almighty and most gracious protection the persons of us thy servants, and the Fleet in which we serve. Preserve us from the dangers of the sea, and from the violence of the enemy; that we may be a safeguard unto our most gracious Sovereign Lady, Queen Elizabeth, and her Dominions, and a security for such as pass on the seas upon their lawful occasions; that the inhabitants of our Island may in peace and quietness serve thee our God; and that we may return in safety to enjoy the blessings of the land, with the fruits of our labours, and with a thankful remembrance of thy mercies to praise and glorify thy holy Name; through Jesus Christ our Lord.

Robert Sanderson, Bishop of Lincoln, Forms of Prayer to be Used at Sea

The manifestation of Christ

152 O GOD, whose blessed Son was manifested that he might destroy the works of the devil, and make us the sons of God and heirs of eternal life: grant us, we beseech thee, that having this hope, we may purify ourselves, even as he is pure; that, when he shall appear again with power and great glory, we may be made like unto him in his eternal and

glorious kingdom; where with thee, O Father, and thee, O Holy Ghost, he liveth and reigneth, ever one God, world without end.

Collect of the Sixth Sunday after the Epiphany

★　★　★

For the fruits of the earth

ALMIGHTY God, Lord of heaven and earth, in whom we live and move and have our being; who doest good unto all men, making thy sun to rise on the evil and on the good, and sending rain on the just and the unjust: favourably behold us thy servants who call upon thy Name, and send us thy blessings from heaven, in giving us fruitful seasons and satisfying us with food and gladness; that both our hearts and mouths may be continually filled with thy praise, and we may ever give thanks to thee in thy holy Church; through Jesus Christ our Lord.

153

John Cosin, 1595–1672, Bishop of Durham

For health of body

O GOD, the Father of lights, from whom cometh down every good and perfect gift: mercifully look upon our frailty and infirmity, and grant us such health of body as thou knowest to be needful for us; that both in body and soul we may evermore serve thee with all our strength; through Jesus Christ our Lord.

154

Bishop Cosin

For our children

155   ALMIGHTY God and heavenly Father, we thank thee for the children which thou hast given us: give us also grace to train them in thy faith, fear and love; that as they advance in years they may grow in grace, and may hereafter be found in the number of thine elect children; through Jesus Christ our Lord.

Bishop Cosin

For holiness

156   O LORD Jesus, who camest down from heaven to redeem us from all iniquity, we beseech thee to write thy word in our hearts that we may know thee, and the power of thy resurrection, and express it in turning from our iniquities. Rule in our hearts by faith, that being dead unto sin and living unto righteousness, we may have our fruit unto holiness and grow in grace and in the practical knowledge of thee.

Henry Hammond, 1605–60, Chaplain to Charles I

In sickness and in health

157   LORD, teach me the art of patience whilst I am well, and give me the use of it when I am sick. In that day either lighten my burden or strengthen my back. Make me, who so often in my health have

discovered my weakness presuming on my own strength, to be strong in my sickness when I solely rely on thy assistance.

Thomas Fuller, 1608–61

Praise and prayer

ETERNAL Lord God, since thy glory and honour is the great end of all thy works, so may it be the beginning and end of all our prayers and services.   158

Let thy great Name be glorified and sanctified throughout the world.

Let the knowledge of thee fill all the earth as the waters cover the sea.

Let that be done in the world which may most advance thy glory.

Let thy wisdom, power, justice, goodness, mercy, and truth be evident unto all mankind, that they may acknowledge and admire it, and magnify the Name of thee, the Eternal God.

Sir Matthew Hale, 1609–77, Lord Chief Justice

Supplication

FAR be it, most gracious Father, from our hearts to harbour anything that is displeasing to thee; let them be temples dedicated to thy service, thoroughly purged from every idol.   159

Let our most gracious King and Redeemer dwell and reign within us, and take full possession of us by his Spirit.

May he extend his peaceable and saving kingdom throughout the whole habitable world.

Let the nations acknowledge their King, and the isles be glad in him, particularly those which we inhabit; and that they may be truly blessed in him, may they submit more dutifully and perfectly to his golden sceptre and the holy laws of his gospel; through Jesus Christ our Lord.

Robert Leighton, 1611–84, Archbishop of Glasgow

Dedication

160   GRANT, O Lord, that I may be so ravished in the wonder of thy love that I may forget myself and all things; may feel neither prosperity nor adversity; may not fear to suffer all the pain in the world rather than be parted from thee.

O let me find thee more inwardly and verily present with me than I am with myself; and make me most circumspect how I do use myself in the presence of thee, my holy Lord.

Archbishop Leighton

For offenders against the law

DELIVER, O most merciful God, those erring 161
ones of thy flock who have fallen into sin.
Remember not their offences, but set them free
from the snare of the enemy. Prosper with the help
of thy Holy Spirit the endeavours of all who are
seeking to train them for good; and grant that being
made partakers of thy heavenly wisdom, they may
be strengthened to the performance of thy laws;
through Jesus Christ our Lord.

Archbishop Leighton

PRAYERS OF BISHOP JEREMY TAYLOR, 1613–67

For the nation

ETERNAL God, who rulest in the kingdoms of 162
men, grant, we most humbly beseech thee,
honour and safety to our Sovereign Lady, Queen
Elizabeth, peace throughout the Commonwealth of
her peoples; promotion to true religion; encouragement to learning and godly living; a patient service
to the concord of the world; and, by all these, glory
to thy holy Name; for the sake of our Lord and
Saviour Jesus Christ.

For the Church

163 PRESERVE, O God, the Catholic Church in holiness and truth, in unity and peace, free from persecution, or glorious under it; that she may advance the honour of her Lord Jesus Christ, for ever represent his sacrifice, and glorify his person, and advance his religion, and be accepted of thee in her blessed Lord; that being filled with his Spirit she may partake of his glory.

For total sanctification

164 O ETERNAL God, who hast made all things subject to man, and man for thy glory: sanctify our souls and bodies, our thoughts and our intentions, our words and actions. Let our body be the servant of our spirit, and both body and spirit servants of Jesus; that doing all things for thy glory here, we may be partakers of thy glory hereafter; through Jesus Christ our Lord.

For faithfulness

165 ENABLE us, O Lord God, to walk in thy way with integrity and cheerfulness, faithfully believing thy Word and faithfully doing thy commandments, faithfully worshipping thee and faithfully serving our neighbour; in the Name of thy Son our Saviour Jesus Christ.

For steadfastness

LORD God, let no riches make me ever to forget   166
myself, no poverty make me to forget thee; let
no hope or fear, no pleasure or pain, no accident
without, no weakness within, hinder my duty, or
turn me from the ways of thy commandments. Let
thy Spirit dwell with me for ever, and make my soul
just and charitable, resolute and constant in holy
purposes, but inflexible to evil.

For our friends

BE pleased, O Lord, to remember our friends: all   167
that have prayed for us and that have done us
good. Do thou good to them, and return all their
kindness double into their own bosom, rewarding
them with blessings, sanctifying them with thy
graces, and bringing them to glory; through Jesus
Christ our Lord.

For those in special need

RELIEVE and comfort, O Lord, all the persecuted   168
and afflicted; speak peace to troubled con-
sciences; strengthen the weak; confirm the strong;
instruct the ignorant; deliver the oppressed from
him that spoilest him; relieve the needy that hath no
helper; and bring us all, by the waters of comfort
and in the ways of righteousness, to thy kingdom of
rest and glory; through Jesus Christ our Lord.

For our children

169 HEAVENLY Father, bless our children with health-ful bodies, with good understandings, with the graces and gifts of thy Spirit, with sweet disposi-tions and holy habits; and sanctify them throughout in their bodies, souls, and spirits, and keep them blameless to the coming of our Lord Jesus Christ.

NOTE *Jeremy Taylor, Bishop of the Irish diocese of Down, Connor and Dromore, is remembered chiefly for his devotional writings, especially for his 'Holy Living and Holy Dying'.*

★ ★ ★

Before Holy Communion

170 GOD our Father, bestow upon us such a measure of thy grace as may sanctify for ever our body and soul which we offer to thee, and may likewise help us to perform those services which we do now promise; through Jesus Christ our Lord.

Daniel Brevint, 1616–85, Dean of Lincoln

For holiness

171 SEND down, O Lord, the Spirit of power into our hearts, and enable us to subdue all unruly passions, to mortify all lusts and desires, and to deny ourselves; that what thou determinest may be our choice, and thy will be the rule of all our actions; through Jesus Christ our Lord.

Anthony Sparrow, 1612–85, Bishop of Exeter

Life's purpose

MY Lord, I have nothing to do in this world but   172
to seek and serve thee.

I have nothing to do with my heart and its affections but to breathe after thee.

I have nothing to do with my tongue and pen but to speak to thee and for thee, and to publish thy glory and thy will.

Richard Baxter, 1615–91, Puritan preacher and divine

Readiness for Christ's coming

KEEP us, O Lord, while we tarry on this earth, in a   173
serious seeking after thee, and in an affectionate
walking with thee, every day of our lives; that when thou comest, we may be found not hiding our talent, nor serving the flesh, nor yet asleep with our lamp unfurnished, but waiting and longing for our Lord, our glorious King, for ever and ever.

Richard Baxter

For loyal service

GIVE us, O Lord, a mind after thine own heart,   174
that we may delight to do thy will; and let thy
law be written in our hearts. Give us courage and resolution to do our duty, and a life spent in thy

service, and in doing all the good we can, in the few remaining days of our pilgrimage here on earth. Grant this for the sake of Jesus Christ thy Son our Lord.

John Tillotson, 1630–94, Archbishop of Canterbury

For the suffering and distressed

175 LORD, who dost not willingly afflict the children of men, behold from thy holy habitation the multitude of suffering souls amongst us.

Have mercy on all ignorant souls and instruct them; on all deluded minds and enlighten them; on all broken hearts and heal them; on all struggling with temptation and rescue them; on all that have fallen from thee and raise them.

O blessed Jesus, who didst shed thy blood for our souls to save them, shed thy Holy Spirit on all and heal them; for thy pity's sake.

William Brough, d. 671, Dean of Gloucester

After Holy Communion

176 O GOD, who hast so greatly loved us, long sought us, and mercifully redeemed us, give us grace that in everything we may yield ourselves, our wills and our works, a continual thankoffering to thee; through Jesus Christ our Lord.

Westminster Confession of Faith, 1647

For the people of Wales

O LORD God, God of gods, great and to be feared, who knowest the secrets of the hearts of all people, and who knowest that my heart's desire for my dear nation according to the flesh is that they may be saved. For thou dost bear witness that many of them have a zeal for God, but not according to knowledge since they know not the Scriptures.

177

Therefore, from the riches of thy mercy, thou dost now send thy Word in fullness among them. Send them also, O Lord, thankful and willing hearts to receive it with all joy and readiness of mind, and to take full account of it; that it may succeed through thy blessing in that for which thou didst send it.

Listen, Lord, from thy dwelling place in heaven to the prayer of thy poor servant, and grant to me and to my nation the requests of my lips; for the sake of thy dear Son, Jesus my Redeemer and Saviour.

Oliver Thomas, the Lover of the People of Wales, 1631

For the coming of the kingdom

L ORD, may your kingdom come among us, so that you as King may rule our hearts with your divine Spirit, and that we as obedient subjects may accept your rule. Be to us our God and let us be your people; you as a Father and we as children; you as Lord and we as servants; you commanding and we obeying; you prohibiting and we refraining; so that we may do your will on earth as the angels do in

178

heaven: not in one thing but in all things, not
fleetingly but for ever, not grudgingly but willingly;
so that your Name may be glorified on earth as it is
in heaven.

Rhys Prichard, d. 1644; tr. W. Rhys Nicholas

PRAYERS OF FAMOUS MEN AND WOMEN
of the period

179

GIVE me my scallop-shell of quiet,
My staff of faith to walk upon;
My scrip of joy, immortal diet;
My bottle of salvation;
My gown of glory (hope's true gage);
And thus I'll take my pilgrimage.

Sir Walter Raleigh, 1552–1618

180

O GOD! thy arm was here;
And not to us, but to thy arm alone,
Ascribe we all.

William Shakespeare, 1564–1616, King Henry V, after Agincourt

181

O THOU, whose captain I account myself . . .
To thee I do commend my watchful soul,
Ere I let fall the windows of mine eyes;
Sleeping or waking, O defend me still.

William Shakespeare, 'Richard III'

O ETERNAL God, and most merciful Father in   182
Jesus Christ, stay not the course of thy mercies
and loving-kindness towards us, but continually
guide our feet in the paths of thy righteousness, and
in the ways of thy commandments; that through thy
grace we may be enabled to lead a godly, holy,
sober, and Christian life in true sincerity and up-
rightness of heart before thee. And that, O Lord, not
for any merits of ours, but only for the merits of thy
Son our Saviour Jesus Christ.

Francis Bacon, Viscount St Albans, 1560–1626

S TRENGTHEN us, O God, to relieve the oppressed,   183
to hear the groans of poor prisoners, to reform
the abuses of all professions; that many be made not
poor to make a few rich; for Jesus Christ's sake.

From a letter of Oliver Cromwell, 1599–1658

O LORD, the Governor of all things, set bounds to   184
our passions by reason, to our errors by truth,
to our discontents by good laws justly executed, and
to our divisions by charity; that we may be, as thy
Jerusalem, a country at unity in itself. Grant this, O
God, in thy good time and for ever, for Christ's
sake.

King Charles I, 1600–49

185 ALMIGHTY and most merciful Father, look down upon us thy unworthy servants through the mediation and merits of Jesus Christ, in whom only thou art well pleased. Purify our hearts by thy Holy Spirit, and as thou dost add days to our lives, so good Lord, we beseech thee to add repentance to our days; that when we have passed this mortal life we may be partakers of thine everlasting kingdom; through the merits of Jesus Christ our Lord.

King Charles I

186 ALMIGHTY and eternal God, the disposer of all the affairs of the world, there is not one circumstance so great as not to be subject to thy power, nor so small but it comes within thy care.

Thy goodness and wisdom show themselves through all thy works, and thy loving-kindness and mercy appear in the several dispensations of thy providence.

May we readily submit ourselves to thy pleasure, and sincerely resign our wills to thine, with all patience, meekness and humility; through Jesus Christ our Lord.

Queen Anne, 1665–1714

187 O LORD, in confidence of thy great mercy and goodness to all that truly repent and resolve to do better, I most humbly implore the grace and assistance of the Holy Spirit to enable me to become every day better.

Grant me the wisdom and understanding to know my duty, and the heart and will to do it.

Endue me, O Lord, with the true fear and love of thee, and with a prudent zeal for thy glory.

Increase in me the graces of charity and meekness, of truth and justice, of humility and patience, and a firmness of spirit to bear every condition with constancy and equality of mind.

King William III, 1650–1702

O GOD, bless and preserve thy Church dispersed 188 over the face of the earth.

Restore to it unity and concord, in the acknowledgement of the Truth and the practice of righteousness.

Remove out of it all errors and dissensions, that they who profess the same Faith may no longer persecute and destroy one another, but be kind and tender hearted one towards another, as it becomes brethren and those that are heirs of the same common salvation.

King William III

NOTHING has been capable, dear Lord, to hinder 189 thee from being all mine, neither heaven, nor your divinity, nor the gibbet of the cross. Grant me thy grace that nothing may hinder me from being all thine, to whom I owe myself both by creation and redemption.

Lady Lucy Herbert, 1669–1744

190   THOU art never weary, O Lord, of doing us good; let us never be weary of doing thee service. But, as thou hast pleasure in the prosperity of thy servants, let us take pleasure in the service of our Lord, and abound in thy work and in thy love and praise evermore.

John Wesley, 1703–91

191   O LORD, take thou full possession of my heart, raise there thy throne, and command there as thou dost in heaven.

   Being created by thee, let me live to thee.
   Being created for thee, let me ever act for thy
      glory.
   Being redeemed by thee, let me render to thee
      what is thine.
And let my spirit cleave to thee alone, for thy
      name's sake.

John Wesley

ALMIGHTY God, in whose hands are all the   192
powers of men, grant that we may not lavish
away the life which thou hast given us on useless
trifles; but enable us by thy Holy Spirit so to shun
sloth and negligence that every day we may dis-
charge the task which thou hast allotted us, and
obtain such success as will most promote thy glory;
for the sake of Jesus Christ.

Dr Samuel Johnson, 1709–84, lexicographer

O GOD, who hast ordained that whatever is to be   193
desired should be sought by labour, look with
mercy on all our studies and endeavours. Grant us,
O Lord, to design only what is lawful and right;
afford us calmness of mind and steadiness of purpose; that we may so do thy will in this short life as
to obtain happiness in the world to come; for the
sake of Jesus Christ our Lord.

Dr Johnson

O GOD, who by love alone art great and glorious,   194
who art present and livest with us by love
alone: grant us likewise by love to attain another
self, by love to live in others, and by love to come to
our glory, to see and accompany thy love throughout all eternity.

Thomas Traherne, 1636–74, metaphysical writer

★   ★   ★

The death of a child

195 MAY we become as this little child who now
follows the Child Jesus, that Lamb of God,
whithersoever he goes; even so, Lord Jesus. Thou
gavest *him* to us, thou hast taken *him* from us.
Blessed be the Name of the Lord. Blessed be our
God for ever and ever.

John Evelyn, 1620–1706, diarist

Doxology

196 To God the Father, who first loved us, and made
us accepted in the Beloved;
To God the Son, who loved us, and washed us
from our sins in his own blood;
To God the Holy Ghost, who sheds the love of
God abroad in our hearts,
Be all love and all glory,
For time and for eternity.

Thomas Ken, 1637–1711, Bishop of Bath and Wells

For the Church's peace and unity

197 O LORD our God, amidst the deplorable divisions
of thy Church, let us never widen its breaches,
but give us universal charity to all who are called by
thy Name. Deliver us from the sins and errors, the
schisms and heresies of the age. O give us grace to
pray for the peace of thy Church, and earnestly to

seek it and to excite all we can to praise and to love thee; through Jesus Christ, our Saviour and Redeemer.

Bishop Ken

*　　*　　*

For a lively faith

LET us not rest, O Lord, in a dead, ineffectual faith, but grant that it may be such as may show itself in good works, enabling us to overcome the world and to conform to the image of the Christ in whom we believe; for his Name's sake.

198

Dean Lancelot Addison, 1632–1707

Trust

TEACH us, O gracious Lord, to begin our works with fear, to go on with obedience, and to finish them in love; and then to wait patiently in hope, and with cheerful confidence to look up to thee, whose promises are faithful and rewards infinite; through Jesus Christ.

199

George Hickes, 1642–1715, Bishop of Thetford

Praise and prayer

ALMIGHTY and most merciful Father, to whose tender compassion we owe our safety in days past, together with all the comforts of this present

200

life, and the hopes of that which is to come: we praise thee, O God, our Creator: unto thee do we give thanks, O God, our exceeding joy, who daily pourest thy benefits upon us.

Leave us not nor forsake us, O Father, but conduct us safe through all changes of our condition here, in holy tranquillity of mind in thy love to us, till we come to dwell with thee and rejoice in thee for ever.

Simon Patrick, 1626–1707, Bishop of Chichester

The departed

201 WE give them back to thee, dear Lord, who gavest them to us. Yet as thou didst not lose them in giving, so we have not lost them by their return. What thou gavest thou takest not away, O Lover of souls; for what is thine is ours also if we are thine.

And life is eternal and love is immortal, and death is only an horizon, and an horizon is nothing save the limit of our sight.

Lift us up, strong Son of God, that we may see further; cleanse our eyes that we may see more clearly; and draw us closer to thyself that we may know ourselves to be nearer to our loved ones who are with thee.

And while thou dost prepare a place for us, prepare us also for that happy place, that where they are and thou art, we too may be for evermore.

William Penn, 1644–1718

Verdict on the Holy Scriptures

L ORD, thou thyself with thine own blest mouth,   202
hast taught thy Word;
   thy Apostles with their blood have confirmed it;
   thy Churches in all ages have set their seal to it;
   thy providence hath watched over it;
   thy power hath preserved and transmitted it pure
     and uncorrupt to us.

Justly dost thou require our assent to this thy
Word, and our highest love and valuation of it.

James Bonnell, 1653–99, Irish Accountant-General

A morning prayer

W AKEN our drowsy heads, O Lord, that early in   203
the morning we may rise to seek thee.

Raise up our sluggish hearts, that we may prepare our richest spices of prayer and devotion to
present to thee.

Let us not lose our courage for any difficulty we
meet with in our way, but hope in our Lord and go
on in our duty.

We know that thou wilt rather work a miracle,
which thy power can do, than forsake thy servants,
which thy goodness cannot.

James Bonnell

Our daily life

204 O LORD, lift up the light of thy countenance upon us; let thy peace rule in our hearts, and may it be our strength and our song in the house of our pilgrimage. We commit ourselves to thy care and keeping; let thy grace be mighty in us, and sufficient for us, in all the duties of the day. Keep us from sin. Give us the rule over our own spirits, and guard us from speaking unadvisedly with our lips. May we live together in holy love and peace, and do thou command thy blessing upon us, even life for evermore.

Matthew Henry, 1662–1714, Nonconformist Bible commentator

The Kingdom of God

205 E NLARGE thy Kingdom, O God, and deliver the world from the tyranny of Satan. Hasten the time, which thy Spirit hath foretold, when all nations whom thou hast made shall worship thee and glorify thy Name. Bless the good endeavours of those who strive to propagate the truth, and prepare the hearts of all men to receive it; to the honour of thy Name.

Thomas Wilson, 1663–1755, Bishop of Sodor and Man

Forgiveness

FORGIVE me my sins, O Lord; the sins of my 206
present and the sins of my past, the sins of my
soul and the sins of my body, the sins which I have
done to please myself and the sins which I have done
to please others. Forgive me my casual sins and my
deliberate sins, and those which I have laboured so
to hide that I have hidden them even from myself.
Forgive me them, O Lord, forgive them all; for Jesus
Christ's sake.

Bishop Wilson

Before prayer

O ALMIGHTY God, the searcher of all hearts, who 207
hast declared that all such as shall draw nigh to
thee with their lips when their hearts are far from
thee are an abomination unto thee: cleanse, we
beseech thee, the thoughts of our hearts by the
inspiration of thy Holy Spirit, that no wandering,
vain, nor idle thoughts may put out of our minds
that reverence and godly fear that becomes all those
who come into thy presence.

Jonathan Swift, 1667–1745, Irish satirist, Dean of St Patrick's, Dublin

After prayer

O GRACIOUS Lord, since thou hast promised that, 208
where two or three are gathered together in thy
Name, thou wilt be in the midst of them to grant

their requests: grant to us who are met in thy Name that those requests which in the utmost sincerity of our hearts we have now made, may effectually be answered; through the merits of Jesus Christ our Lord.

Dean Swift

For love

209   O GOD, in whom nothing can live but as it lives in love, grant us the spirit of love which does not want to be rewarded, honoured or esteemed, but only to become the blessing and happiness of everything that wants it; love which is the very joy of life, and thine own goodness and truth within the soul; who thyself art Love, and by love our Redeemer, from eternity to eternity.

William Law, 1686–1761, spiritual writer

Prayers in hymns for life's pilgrimage

210   O GOD of Bethel, by whose hand
     Thy people still are fed;
Who through this weary pilgrimage
     Hast all our fathers led:

Our vows, our prayers, we now present
     Before thy throne of grace;
God of our fathers, be the God
     Of their succeeding race.

Through each perplexing path of life
　Our wandering footsteps guide;
Give us each day our daily bread,
　And raiment fit provide.

O spread thy covering wings around,
　Till all our wanderings cease,
And at our Father's loved abode
　Our souls arrive in peace.

Philip Doddridge, 1702–51, as in 'Scottish Paraphrases', 1781

Guide me, O thou great Jehovah,
　Pilgrim through this barren land;
I am weak, but thou art mighty,
　Hold me with thy powerful hand;
　　Bread of heaven,
Feed me till I want no more.

Open now the crystal fountain
　Whence the healing stream doth flow;
Let the fire and cloudy pillar
　Lead me all my journey through;
　　Strong Deliverer,
Be thou still my strength and shield.

When I tread the verge of Jordan,
　Bid my anxious fears subside;
Death of death, and hell's destruction,
　Land me safe on Canaan's side;
　　Songs of praises
I will ever give to thee.

William Williams, 1716–91, 'the sweet singer of Wales'

211

A prayer for unity

212   O GOD, the Father of our Lord Jesus Christ, our only Saviour, the Prince of Peace, give us grace seriously to lay to heart the great dangers we are in by our unhappy divisions. Take away all hatred and prejudice, and whatsoever else may hinder us from godly union and concord; that as there is but one Body, and one Spirit, and one Hope of our Calling, one Lord, one Faith, one Baptism, one God and Father of us all, so we may henceforth be all of one heart and of one soul, united in one holy bond of Truth and Peace, of Faith and Charity, and may with one mind and one mouth glorify thee; through Jesus Christ our Lord.

Accession Service, 1715

For the Sovereign

213   O GOD, who providest for thy people by thy power, and rulest over them in love: vouchsafe so to bless thy servant our Queen, that under her this nation may be wisely governed, and thy Church may serve thee in all godly quietness; and grant that she being devoted to thee with her whole heart, and persevering in good works unto the end, may, by thy guidance, come to thine everlasting kingdom; through Jesus Christ thy Son our Lord, who liveth and reigneth with thee and the Holy Ghost, ever one God, world without end.

Accession Service

Watching for the Lord

O THOU, who hast foretold that thou wilt return   214
to judgment in an hour that we are not aware
of: grant us grace to watch and pray always; that
whether thou shalt come at even, or at midnight, or
in the morning, we may be found among the number of those servants who shall be blessed in watching for their Lord; to whom be all glory, now and
for evermore.

Non-Jurors' Prayers Book, 1734

Supplication

O THAT I may continue to drink deep of the   215
streams of the great salvation, until I wholly
lose the thirst for the passing things of earth; to live
watching for my Lord, to be wide awake when
he comes, to open to him quickly, and enjoy his
likeness to the full.

Ann Griffiths, eighteenth-century Welsh hymn-writer

For sincerity

O LORD, I do not wish to be a hypocrite,   216
deceiving myself.
You know all things, you know the roots of my
heart.
If my heart does not seek you, Lord, purify me
from guile.
Test me and see if my way is ungodly.

John Thomas, 1730–1804; from Rhad Ras, 1830

For charity

217 GRANT, O God, that we may keep a constant guard upon our thoughts and passions, that they may never lead us into sin; that we may live in perfect charity with all mankind, in affection to those that love us, and in forgiveness to those, if any there are, that hate us. Give us good and virtuous friends. In the Name of our blessed Lord and Saviour Jesus Christ.

Warren Hastings, 1732–1818, Governor-General of Bengal

PRAYERS OF THE POETS
of the period

Judge of the nations

218 THE Lord will come, and not be slow,
　　His footsteps cannot err;
Before him righteousness shall go,
　　His royal harbinger.

Truth from the earth, like to a flower,
　　Shall bud and blossom then;
And justice, from her heavenly bower,
　　Look down on mortal men.

Rise, God, judge thou the earth in might,
　　This wicked earth redress;
For thou art he who shalt by right
　　The nations all possess.

The nations all whom thou hast made
  Shall come, and all shall frame
To bow them low before thee, Lord,
  And glorify thy name.

For great thou art, and wonders great
  By thy strong hand are done:
Thou in thy everlasting seat
  Remainest God alone.

John Milton, 1608–74; based on Psalm 85

We are God's workmanship

VIEW me, Lord, a work of thine: 219
  Shall I then lie drown'd in night?
Might thy grace in me but shine,
  I should seem all made of light.

But my soul still surfeits so
  On the poisoned baits of sin,
That I strange and ugly grow,
  All is dark and foul within.

Cleanse me, Lord, that I may kneel
  At thine altar, pure and white:
They that once thy mercies feel
  Gaze no more on earth's delight.

In thy word, Lord, is my trust,
  To thy mercies fast I fly;
Though I am but clay and dust,
  Yet thy grace can lift me high.

Thomas Campion, 1567–1620

From 'The Litany'

220

HEAR us, O hear us Lord; to thee
    A sinner is more music, when he prays,
Than spheres, or angels' praises be,
    In panegyric alleluias,
    Hear us, for till thou hear us, Lord,
    We know not what to say.
Thine ear to our sighs, tears, thoughts gives voice
    and word.

O thou who Satan heard'st in Job's sick day,
Hear thyself now, for thou in us dost pray.

John Donne, 1572–1631

Coming to God through Christ

221

GOOD and great God! how should I fear
    To come to thee, if Christ not there!
Could I but think he would not be
Present, to plead my cause for me,
To hell I'd rather run, than I
Would see thy face, and he not by.

Robert Herrick, 1591–1674

Grace abounding

IF I have played the truant, or have here
Failed in my part; Oh! thou that art my dear,
My mild, my loving tutor, Lord and God,
Correct my errors gently with thy rod.
I know that faults will many here be found,
But where sin dwells, there let thy grace abound.

Robert Herrick

222

The Elixir: 'for thy sake'

TEACH me, my God and King,
    In all things thee to see,
And what I do in anything,
    To do it as for thee.

All may of thee partake,
    Nothing can be so mean
Which with this tincture, 'for thy sake',
    Will not grow bright and clean.

A servant with this clause
    Makes drudgery divine;
Who sweeps a room as for thy laws
    Makes that and the action fine.

George Herbert, 1593–1633

223

A grateful heart

224

THOU that hast given so much to me,
Give one thing more, a grateful heart.
Not thankful when it pleases me,
As if thy blessings had spare days;
But such a heart whose very pulse
May be thy praise.

George Herbert

'The dear bargain'

225

LORD, what is man? why should he cost thee
So dear? what had his ruin lost thee?
Lord, what is man? that thou hast overbought
So much a thing of nought?

O my Saviour, make me see
How dearly thou hast paid for me,
That lost again my life may prove
As then in death, so now in love.

Richard Crawshaw, 1613–49

God's homely dwelling

226

MY dear, dear God! I do not know
What lodged thee then, nor where, nor how;
But I am sure thou now dost come
Oft to a narrow, homely room,
Where thou too hast but the least part,
My God: I mean my sinful heart.

Henry Vaughan, 1622–95

Universal praise

FROM all that dwell below the skies,   227
Let the Creator's praise arise;
Let the Redeemer's name be sung
Through every land by every tongue.

Eternal are thy mercies, Lord;
Eternal truth attends thy word;
Thy praise shall sound from shore to shore,
Till suns shall rise and set no more.

In every land begin the song;
To every land the strains belong;
In cheerful sounds all voices raise
And fill the world with loudest praise.

Isaac Watts, 1674–1748, the father of English hymnody

The celestial fire

O THOU who camest from above,   228
The pure celestial fire to impart,
Kindle a flame of sacred love
On the mean altar of my heart.

There let it for thy glory burn
With inextinguishable blaze,
And trembling to its source return
In humble prayer and fervent praise.

Jesus, confirm my heart's desire
To work and speak and think for thee;
Still let me guard the holy fire,
And still stir up thy gift in me.

Charles Wesley, 1707–88

A closer walk with God

229

O FOR a closer walk with God,
    A calm and heavenly frame;
A light to shine upon the road
    That leads me to the Lamb!

What peaceful hours I once enjoyed:
    How sweet their memory still!
But they have left an aching void
    The world can never fill.

Return, O holy Dove, return,
    Sweet messenger of rest;
I hate the sins that made thee mourn,
    And drove thee from my breast.

The dearest idol I have known,
    Whate'er that idol be,
Help me to tear it from thy throne,
    And worship only thee.

William Cowper, 1731–1800

In prospect of death

230

O THOU unknown, Almighty Cause
    Of all my hope and fear,
In whose dread Presence, ere an hour,
    Perhaps I must appear!

Thou know'st that thou hast formèd me
    With passions wild and strong;
And listening to their witching voice
    Has often led me wrong.

Where with intention I have erred,
  No other plea I have,
But, thou art Good; and goodness still
  Delighteth to forgive.

Robert Burns, 1759–96.

PART IV

THE GEORGIAN AND VICTORIAN AGE

Sectional Prayers:

Prayers of famous men and women of the period
Prayers of Victorian hymn-writers
Prayers of the poets of the period
Prayers of Bishop Brooke Foss Westcott

4
The Georgian and Victorian age

For God's peace

LORD, teach us to number our days, that we may apply our hearts unto wisdom.

Lighten, if it be thy will, the pressures of this world's cares.

Above all, reconcile us to thy will, and give us a peace which the world cannot take away; through our Saviour Jesus Christ.

Thomas Chalmers, 1780–1847, Scottish divine

For conformity to God's will

SEND out thy light and thy truth, that I may live always near to thee, my God. Let me feel thy love, that I may be as it were already in heaven, that I may do my work as the angels do theirs; and let me be ready for every work, ready to go out or go in, to stay or depart, just as thou shalt appoint.

Lord, let me have no will of my own, or consider my true happiness as depending in the smallest degree on anything that can befall me outwardly, but as consisting altogether in conformity to thy will.

Henry Martyn, 1781–1812, scholar and pioneer missionary to India and Persia

Consecration

233 O JESUS CHRIST, Son of the living God, take, for the sake of thy cruel death, my time and strength, and the gifts and talents I possess: which with a full purpose of heart I consecrate to thy glory in the building up of thy Church in the world; for thou art worthy of the hearts and talents of all men.

Christmas Evans, 1766–1838, Welsh evangelist

For usefulness in Christ's service

234 I DESIRE thee, my great High Priest, to confirm my usefulness as a preacher and my piety as a Christian; that sin may not have place in my heart to becloud my confidence in thy righteousness. May I not be left to any foolish act that may occasion my gifts to wither, and I be rendered useless before my life ends. Keep thy gracious eye upon me, and watch over me, O my Lord and my God, for ever.

Christmas Evans

For true knowledge

235 LORD, give us a heart to turn all knowledge to thy glory and not to our own. Keep us from being deluded with the lights of vain philosophies. Keep us from the pride of human reason. Let us not think

our own thoughts; but in all things acting under the guidance of the Holy Spirit, may we find thee everywhere, and live in all simplicity, humility and singleness of heart unto the Lord.

Henry Kirke White, 1785–1806, poet

In the morning

O GOD, by whom the world is governed and preserved, we thine unworthy servants draw nigh unto thee to offer our morning sacrifice of prayer and praise. May we remember that every day is thy gift, to be used in thy service. Enable us to resist all evil, and dispose us to follow the guidance of thy good Spirit, not trusting to our own strength or wisdom, but looking to thee to establish us in every good word and work; through Jesus Christ our Lord. 236

Charles James Blomfield, 1786–1857, Bishop of London

For a quiet mind

O LORD, this is our desire, to walk along the path of life that thou hast appointed us, in steadfastness of faith, in lowliness of heart, in gentleness of love. Let not the cares or duties of this life press on us too heavily; but lighten our burdens, that we may follow thy way in quietness, filled with thankfulness for thy mercy; through Jesus Christ our Lord. 237

Maria Hare, 1798–1870, parson's wife, Alton Barnes

For cheerfulness

238 O GOD, animate us to cheerfulness. May we have a joyful sense of our blessings, learn to look on the bright circumstances of our lot, and maintain a perpetual contentedness.

Preserve us from despondency and from yielding to dejection. Teach us that nothing can hurt us if, with true loyalty of affection, we keep thy commandments and take refuge in thee.

William E. Channing, 1780–1842

Our daily life and service

239 O LORD Jesus Christ, who when on earth wast ever occupied about thy Father's business: grant that we may not grow weary in well-doing. Give us grace to do all in thy Name.

Be thou the beginning and the end of all: the pattern whom we follow, the Redeemer in whom we trust, the Master whom we serve, the Friend to whom we look for sympathy.

May we never shrink from our duty through any fear of man; make us faithful unto death; and bring us at last into the eternal Presence, where with the Father and the Holy Ghost thou livest and reignest for ever.

Edward Bouverie Pusey, 1800–82, Tractarian leader

The quest for peace

LET us never seek *out* of thee what we can find only   240
in thee, O Lord: peace and rest and joy and bliss,
which abide in thee alone.

Lift up our souls above the weary round of
harassing thoughts to thy eternal presence.

Lift up our minds to the pure, bright, serene
light of thy presence, that there we may repose in
thy love and be at rest from ourselves and all things
that weary us; and thence return, arrayed in thy
peace, to do and to bear whatsoever shall best please
thee, O blessed Lord.

E. B. Pusey

Endurance of suffering

O MY dear Lord, though I am so very weak that I   241
have not strength to ask thee for suffering as a
gift, at least I will beg of thee grace to meet suffering
well when thou in thy love and wisdom dost bring it
upon me. Let me bear pain, reproach, disappoint-
ment, slander, anxiety, suspense, as thou wouldest
have me, O my Jesu, and as thou by thy own
suffering hast taught me, when it comes.

John Henry Newman, Cardinal, 1801–90

Teacher and learner

242 I NEED thee to teach me day by day, according to each day's opportunities and needs.

Give me, O my Lord, that purity of conscience which alone can receive and improve thy inspirations.

My ears are dull, so that I cannot hear thy voice.

My eyes are dim, so that I cannot see thy tokens.

Thou alone canst quicken my hearing, and purge my sight, and cleanse and renew my heart.

Teach me to sit at thy feet, and hear thy word.

Cardinal Newman

For single-mindedness

243 SAVE us, O Lord, from the snares of a double mind.
Deliver us from all cowardly neutralities.
Make us to go in the paths of thy commandments,
and to trust for our defence in thy mighty arm
alone;
through Jesus Christ our Lord.

Richard Hurrell Froude, 1803–36, scholar and Tractarian leader

Unity in the Holy Trinity

Most blessed and glorious Trinity, Three   244
Persons in One God, teach us to worship and
adore that absolute Trinity, that perfect Unity. And
that we may adore thee, that our worship may not
be a mockery, make us to know that we are one in
Christ, as the Father is one with the Son, and the Son
with the Father.

Suffer us not to look upon our sectarianism as if
it were a destiny. Help us to regard it as a rebellion
against thee.

Help us to see all distinctions more clearly in the
light of thy love. Help us to feel and confess the
feebleness of our own efforts.

So may thy holy Name embrace us more and
more, and all creation at last glorify thee throughout all ages.

Frederick Denison Maurice, 1805–72, theologian

For a true knowledge of God

O GOD of our life, whom we dimly apprehend   245
and can never comprehend, to whom never-
theless we justly ascribe all goodness as well as all
greatness: as a Father teaches his children, so teach us
true thoughts of thee. Help us to aspire, as far as man
may lawfully aspire, to a knowledge of thee.

Thou art not only a God to be honoured in times
of rest and ease. Thou art also the refuge of the

distressed, the comforter of the afflicted, the support of the unstable. As we sympathise with those who are smitten by calamity, wounded by sudden accident, wrecked in the midst of security, so must we believe that thy mighty all-embracing heart sympathises far more than we do.

Be thou the stay of all in life and death, and teach us to know thee and trust thee fully; through Jesus Christ our Lord.

Professor Francis William Newman, 1805–97

The solemn trust of life

246   ETERNAL God, who committest to us the swift and solemn trust of life: since we know not what a day may bring forth, but only that the hour for serving thee is always present, may we wake to the instant claims of thy holy will, not waiting till tomorrow but yielding today.

Consecrate with thy presence the way our feet may go, and the humblest work will shine and the roughest places be made plain. In all things draw us to the mind of Christ, that thy lost image may be traced again, and thou mayest own us at one with him and thee, to the glory of thy great name.

Dr James Martineau, 1805–1900, Unitarian divine

For absent friends

O LORD our God, who art in every place, and from whom no space or distance can ever separate us, we know that those who are absent from each other are present with thee. We therefore pray thee to have in thy holy keeping those dear ones from whom we are now parted; and grant that both they and we, by drawing nearer unto thee, may be drawn nearer to each other, bound together by the unseen chain of thy love, in the communion of thy Spirit; through Jesus Christ our Lord.

247

Sir William Martin, 1807–82, first Chief Justice of New Zealand

For an unselfish spirit

O LORD, give us more charity, more self-denial, more likeness to thee. Teach us to sacrifice our comforts to others, and our likings for the sake of doing good. Make us kindly in thought, gentle in word, generous in deed. Teach us that it is better to give than to receive, better to forget ourselves than to put ourselves forward, better to minister than to be ministered unto. And to thee, the God of Love, be all glory and praise, now and for ever.

248

Henry Alford, 1810–71, Dean of Canterbury

The common heart

249

GIVE me an heart that beats
In all its pulses with the common heart
Of human kind, which the same things make glad,
The same make sorry. Give me grace enough
Even in their first beginnings to detect
The endeavours which the proud heart still is
   making
To cut itself from off the common root,
To set itself upon a private base,
To have wherein to glory of its own,
Beside the common glory of the kind!
Each such attempt in all its hateful pride
And meanness, give me to detect and loathe –
A man, and claiming fellowship with men!

Richard Chenevix Trench, 1807–86, Archbishop of Dublin

PRAYERS OF FAMOUS MEN AND WOMEN
of the period

The spirit of prayer

250

GIVE us grace, Almighty Father, to address thee
with all our hearts as well as with our lips.

Thou art everywhere present: from thee no
secrets can be hidden.

Teach us to fix our thoughts on thee, reverently and with love, so that our prayers are not in vain, but are acceptable to thee, now and always; through Jesus Christ our Lord.

Jane Austen, 1775–1817

For the victory of the fleet

MAY the great God, whom I worship, grant to my country, and for the benefit of Europe in general, a great and glorious victory; and may no misconduct in any one tarnish it; and may humanity after victory be the predominant feature in the British fleet.

For myself individually, I commit my life to him that made me, and may his blessing alight on my endeavours for serving my country faithfully.

To him I resign myself, and the just cause which is entrusted to me to defend. Amen. Amen. Amen.

Written by Lord Nelson, 1758–1805, on the eve of Trafalgar, 1805

For our daily work

O LORD, give thy blessing, we pray thee, to our daily work, that we may do it in faith and heartily, as to the Lord and not unto men.

All our powers of body and mind are thine, and we would fain devote them to thy service. Sanctify

251

252

them, and the work in which we are engaged; and do thou, O Lord, so bless our efforts that they may bring forth in us the fruits of true wisdom.

Teach us to seek after truth and enable us to gain it; and grant that while we know earthly things, we may know thee, and be known by thee, through and in thy Son Jesus Christ.

Thomas Arnold, 1795–1842, Headmaster of Rugby School

Our service to others

253 O GOD, the Father of the forsaken, who dost teach us that love towards man is the bond of perfectness and the imitation of thyself: open our eyes and touch our hearts that we may see and do the things which belong to our peace.

Strengthen us in the work which we have undertaken; give us wisdom, perseverance, faith and zeal; and in thine own time and according to thy pleasure prosper the issue; for the love of thy Son Jesus Christ our Lord.

Lord Shaftesbury, 1801–85, social reformer

After Holy Communion

254 GO forth with us, O Lord, from this thy holy house; cast about us the fence which the evil one cannot pass, and clothe us in the armour which his darts cannot pierce. Send down upon us thy love

and light and calm, wherein, as in a cloud, we may continually dwell and worship thee for evermore; through Jesus Christ our Lord.

William Ewart Gladstone, 1809–98

God's faithful servants

GRANT, O God, that we may wait patiently, as servants standing before their Lord, to know thy will; that we may welcome all truth, under whatever outward forms it may be uttered; that we may bless every good deed, by whomsoever it may be done; and that we may rise above all party strife to the contemplation of the eternal Truth and Goodness; through Jesus Christ our Lord.

255

Charles Kingsley, 1819–75

Against pride and vanity

TAKE from us, O God, all pride and vanity, all boasting and forwardness, and give us the true courage that shows itself by gentleness; the true wisdom that shows itself by simplicity; and the true power that shows itself by modesty; through Jesus Christ our Lord.

256

Charles Kingsley

The sinner's Saviour

257 SAVIOUR of sinners! When a poor woman, laden with sins, went out to the well to draw water, she found thee sitting at the well. She knew thee not; she had not sought thee; her mind was dark; her life was unholy. But thou didst speak to her, thou didst teach her, thou didst show her that her life lay open before thee, and yet thou wast ready to give her that blessing which she had never sought.

Jesus! thou knowest all men. If their minds are dark, their lives unholy, if they have come out not seeking thee, not desiring to be taught: deal with them according to the free mercy which thou didst show to her. Speak to them, Lord; bring their sins to their minds, and make them thirst for that salvation which thou art ready to give.

George Eliot, 1819–80, from Dinah Morris's prayer in 'Adam Bede'

For the nation

258 O GOD, the God of all righteousness, mercy and love: give us all grace and strength to conceive and execute whatever be for thine honour and the welfare of the nation; that we may become at last, through the merits and intercession of our common Redeemer, a great and a happy, because a wise and understanding people, to thy honour and glory.

Lord Salisbury, 1830–1903, Prime Minister

Fidelity to God

O LORD God, grant us always, whatever the world may say, to content ourselves with what thou wilt say, and to care only for thine approval, which will outweigh all worlds; for Jesus Christ's sake.

General Charles Gordon, 1833–85, Governor of the Sudan

259

Morning

THE day returns and brings us the petty round of irritating concerns and duties. Help us to play the man, help us to perform them with laughter and kind faces, let cheerfulness abound with industry. Give us to go blithely on our business all this day; bring us to our resting beds weary and content and undishonoured; and grant us in the end the gift of sleep.

Robert Louis Stevenson, 1850–94

260

★   ★   ★

For family and friends

HEAVENLY Father, we beseech thee to look in thy mercy upon this household. Grant that every member of it may be taught and guided of thee. Bless the relations and friends of each of us: thou knowest their several necessities; and prosper our efforts to advance thy kingdom at home and abroad; for our Lord Jesus Christ's sake.

Archibald Campbell Tait, 1811–82, Archbishop of Canterbury

261

For usefulness

262   OUR Father, let us never be without the indwelling of thy Holy Spirit for an hour.

Let our lives be every day more unconscious of our own presence and more conscious of thine.

Make us instruments in thy hand for advancing thy kingdom, and for uniting all Christians in this land in thy one Church; for the sake of him who loved us, and died for us, even Jesus Christ our Saviour.

Norman Macleod, 1812–72, Scottish divine

In time of crisis

263   LOOK in compassion, O heavenly Father, upon this troubled and divided world. Though we cannot trace thy footsteps or understand thy working, give us grace to trust thee with an undoubting faith; and when thine own time is come, reveal, O Lord, that new heaven and new earth wherein dwelleth righteousness, where the Prince of peace ruleth, thy Son our Saviour Jesus Christ.

Charles John Vaughan, 1816–97, Dean of Llandaff

God in daily life

O GOD our Father, who alone satisfiest the desire 264
of every living thing, who ordainest our
strength for thy service, and grantest us intervals of
rest for the renewal of our strength: sanctify, we
beseech thee, to thy glory, our labour and our rest,
our seriousness and our mirth, our sorrow and our
joy; and dismiss us now with thy blessing, that we
may go on our way rejoicing; through Jesus Christ
our Lord.

George, 4th Baron Lyttleton, 1817–76

For Christian usefulness

THOUGH we know not what is good for us, give 265
us, O Lord, what thou seest is best. Only fit us
for what thou givest, and let it bring to our souls
health and peace, with some good to our neighbour
and the world, for thy goodness' sake, O Lord.

Rowland Williams, 1818–70

In time of adversity

O GOD, who makest cheerfulness the companion 266
of strength, but apt to take wings in time of
adversity, we humbly beseech thee that if in thy
sovereign wisdom thou sendest trials, yet for thy
mercy's sake deny us not the comfort of patience.

Lay not more upon us, O heavenly Father, than thou wilt enable us to bear, and grant us that heavenly calmness which comes of owning thy hand in all things; through Jesus Christ.

Rowland Williams

Our work

267 ALMIGHTY God and heavenly Father, who by thy divine providence hast appointed for each one of us our work in life, help us always to remember that our work is thy appointment, and to do it heartily as unto thee. Preserve us from slothfulness, and make us to live with loins girded and lamps burning; that whensoever our Lord may come, we may be found striving earnestly to finish the work that thou hast given us to do; through the same Jesus Christ our Lord.

Edward Meyrick Goulburn, 1818–97, Dean of Norwich

For the parish

268 ALMIGHTY and everlasting God, who dost govern all things in heaven and earth, mercifully hear our prayers and grant to this parish all things needful for its spiritual welfare.

Strengthen and confirm the faithful, visit and relieve the sick, turn and soften the wicked, arouse the careless, recover the fallen, restore the penitent.

Remove all hindrances to the advancement of thy Word, and bring us all to be of one heart and mind in Jesus Christ, to the honour and glory of thy Name.

William John Butler, 1818–94, Dean of Lincoln

For the faithful departed

O LORD, we praise thy holy Name for all thy servants departed from among us in thy faith and fear; and we humbly beseech thee so to bless us who remain on earth that, being protected from all evil, we may ever serve and please thee with quiet minds and thankful hearts, and together with those that are gone before may have our refreshment in paradise and our portion in the resurrection of the just; through Jesus Christ our Saviour.

269

Frederick Temple, 1821–1902, Archbishop of Canterbury

The appeal of the Cross

O LORD Jesu Christ, take us to thyself, draw us with cords to the foot of thy cross; for we have no strength to come, and we know not the way. Thou art mighty to save, and none can separate us from thy love. Bring us home to thyself, for we are gone astray. We have wandered: do thou seek us. Under the shadow of thy cross let us live all the rest of our lives, and there we shall be safe.

270

Archbishop Frederick Temple

Men for the ministry

271 O LORD, we beseech thee to raise up for the work of the ministry faithful and able men, counting it all joy to spend and be spent for the sake of thy dear Son, and for the souls for which he shed his most precious blood; and we pray thee to fit them for their holy function by thy bountiful grace and heavenly benediction, for thy honour and glory.

Edward White Benson, 1829–96, Archbishop of Canterbury

Teach me, good Lord

272 TEACH me, good Lord, not to murmur at multitude of business or shortness of time;

not to magnify undertaken duties by seeming to suffer under them, but to treat all as liberties and gladnesses;

not to call attention to crowded work, or petty fatigues;

not to gather encouragement from appreciation from others, lest this should interfere with purity of motive;

not to seek respect or regard from superiors on account of age or past service.

Archbishop Benson

For light

WE give thee thanks, Almighty God, for that 273
inward light by which in the midst of outward
darkness we may behold, as far as may be, thy
purposes and thy doings, and see under all things
thy judgments; that being upheld by perfect trust in
thee, we may be fearless in times of darkness, and
pass on through life in safety, guided by thy light;
for thy mercy in Jesus Christ our Lord.

George Dawson, 1821–76, Nonconformist minister

Students for the ministry

O EVERLASTING God, who art ever adored by the 274
holy angels, yet dost choose men to be the
stewards of thy mysteries: bless, we beseech thee,
all thy servants who are preparing and training
for the Church's ministry; that they who cannot
do anything good without thee, may by thee be
illuminated with a true knowledge of thy Word
and Sacraments; and that being made able ministers of the new covenant they may advance thy
glory and the salvation of souls; through Jesus
Christ our Lord.

Henry Parry Liddon, 1829–90, Canon of St Paul's

The clergy

275 O LORD, who makest thine angels spirits, and thy ministers a flame of fire: vouchsafe, we beseech thee, to stir up and confirm the sacred grace of Orders in all stewards of thy mysteries; that as ministering spirits they may gather out of thy kingdom all things that offend, and may kindle in the hearts of all that fire which thou camest to send upon the earth; who livest and reignest with the Father and the Holy Ghost, ever one God, world without end.

Canon Liddon

For acceptable worship

276 ALMIGHTY God, from whom every good prayer cometh, and who pourest out on all who desire it the spirit of grace and supplication: deliver us, when we draw nigh to thee, from coldness of heart and wandering of mind; that with steadfast thoughts and kindled affections we may worship thee in spirit and in truth; through Jesus Christ our Lord.

William Bright, 1824–1901, Church historian

For church workers

277 O LORD, without whom our labour is but lost, and with whom thy little ones go forth as the mighty: be present in all works in thy Church which are undertaken according to thy will; and grant to

thy labourers a pure intention, patient faith, sufficient success upon earth, and the bliss of serving thee in heaven; through Jesus Christ our Lord.

William Bright

For guidance

O GOD, by whom the meek are guided in judgment, and light riseth up in darkness for the godly: grant us, in all our doubts and uncertainties, the grace to ask what thou wouldest have us to do; that the Spirit of wisdom may save us from all false choices, and that in thy light we may see light; through Jesus Christ our Lord. 278

William Bright

PRAYERS OF VICTORIAN
HYMN-WRITERS

A missionary prayer

O SPIRIT of the living God, 279
 In all the fullness of thy grace,
Where'er the foot of man hath trod,
 Descend on our apostate race.

Give tongues of fire and hearts of love
 To preach the reconciling word;
Give power and wisdom from above,
 Where'er the joyful sound is heard.

Be darkness, at thy coming, light,
  Confusion, order in thy path;
Souls without strength inspire with might,
  Bid mercy triumph over wrath.

Baptise the nations; far and nigh
  The triumphs of the cross record;
The name of Jesus glorify,
  Till every kindred call him Lord.

James Montgomery, 1771–1854, Sheffield journalist

Life's eventide

280

ABIDE with me; fast falls the eventide;
  The darkness deepens; Lord, with me abide;
When other helpers fail, and comforts flee,
Help of the helpless, O abide with me.

Swift to its close ebbs out life's little day;
Earth's joys grow dim, its glories pass away;
Change and decay in all around I see;
O thou who changest not, abide with me.

I fear no foe with thee at hand to bless;
Ills have no weight, and tears no bitterness;
Where is death's sting? where, grave, thy victory?
I triumph still, if thou abide with me.

Hold thou thy Cross before my closing eyes;
Shine through the gloom, and point me to the
    skies;
Heaven's morning breaks, and earth's vain
    shadows flee;
In life, in death, O Lord, abide with me.

Henry Francis Lyte, 1793–1847

Life's praises

FILL thou my life, O Lord my God,   281
    In every part with praise,
That my whole being may proclaim
    Thy being and thy ways.

Not for the lip of praise alone,
    Nor e'en the praising heart
I ask, but for a life made up
    Of praise in every part.

Praise in the common things of life,
    Its goings out and in;
Praise in each duty and each deed,
    However small and mean.

So shalt thou, gracious Lord, from me
    Receive the glory due;
And so shall I begin on earth
    The song for ever new.

Horatius Bonar, 1808–89, known as the prince of Scottish hymn-writers

At the Holy Communion

I AM not worthy, holy Lord,   282
    That thou shouldst come to me;
Speak but the word: one gracious word
    Can set the sinner free.

I am not worthy: cold and bare
    The lodging of my soul;
How canst thou deign to enter there?
    Lord, speak, and make me whole.

I am not worthy: yet, my God,
   How can I say thee nay?
Thee, who didst give thy flesh and blood
   My ransom price to pay?

O come in this sweet morning hour,
   Feed me with food divine;
And fill with all thy love and power
   This worthless heart of mine.

Sir Henry Williams Baker, 1821–77, promoter and first editor of
'Hymns Ancient and Modern', 1861

The kingdom of God

283

THY kingdom come, O God,
   Thy rule, O Christ, begin;
Break with thine iron rod
   The tyrannies of sin.

Where is thy reign of peace,
   Of purity and love?
When shall all hatred cease,
   As in the realms above?

When comes the promised time
   That war shall be no more,
And lust, oppression, crime,
   Shall flee thy face before?

We pray thee, Lord, arise,
   And come in thy great might;
Revive our longing eyes,
   Which languish for thy sight.

O'er heathen lands afar
   Thick darkness broodeth yet;
Arise, O Morning Star,
   Arise, and never set.

Lewis Hensley, 1824–1905, senior Cambridge mathematician

Consecration

TAKE my life, and let it be   284
  Consecrated, Lord, to thee;
Take my moments and my days,
Let them flow in ceaseless praise.

Take my hands, and let them move
At the impulse of thy love;
Take my feet, and let them be
Swift and beautiful for thee.

Take my voice, and let me sing
Always, only, for my King;
Take my lips, and let them be
Filled with messages from thee.

Take my love; my Lord I pour
At thy feet its treasure-store;
Take myself, and I will be
Ever, only, all for thee.

Frances Ridley Havergal, 1836–79

★   ★   ★

Evangelism

285 O LORD Jesus Christ, great shepherd of the sheep, who seekest those that are gone astray, bindest up those that are broken, and healest those that are sick: bless, we beseech thee, all efforts that are made to convert souls unto thee. Open the deaf ears of the wandering, that they may hear the words which belong unto their peace; and grant that those whom thou dost raise to newness of life may through thy grace persevere unto the end, of thy mercy, blessed Lord, to whom with the Father and the Holy Spirit be all praise and glory.

After Richard Meux Benson, 1824–1915, founder of the
Cowley Brotherhood

For the rich and influential

286 WE beseech thee, O Lord, that all those to whom thou hast given positions of influence may praise thee in their lives, honour thee with their wealth, and induce others by their example to seek that incorruptible inheritance which thy beloved Son hath promised to all who follow him in meekness, and purity, and faith.

R. M. Benson

For humility

O LORD Jesus Christ, who didst humble thyself
to become man, and to be born into the world
for our salvation: teach us the grace of humility, root
out of our hearts all pride and haughtiness, and so
fashion us after thy holy likeness in this world, that
in the world to come we may be made like unto thee
in thy eternal kingdom.

287

William Walsham How, 1823–97, first Bishop of Wakefield

For renewed zeal

M OST merciful Father, we confess that we have
done little to forward thy kingdom and
advance thy glory. Pardon our shortcomings and
give us greater zeal for thy service. Make us more
ready and diligent by our prayers, by our alms, and
by our examples, to spread the knowledge of thy
truth and to enlarge the boundaries of thy kingdom;
and may we do all to thy glory.

288

Bishop How

Remembrance of the Cross

O LORD, do thou, in thy great mercy, keep us
from forgetting what thou hast suffered for us
in body and soul. May we never be drawn by the
cares of this life from Jesus our Friend and Saviour,
but daily may we live nearer to his cross.

289

Captain Hedley Vicars, b. 1826, killed at Sebastopol, 1855

The faithful departed

290 O THOU Lord of all worlds, we bless thy Name for all those who have entered into their rest, and reached the promised land where thou art seen face to face. Give us grace to follow in their footsteps, as they followed in the footsteps of thy holy Son.

Keep alive in us the memory of those dear to ourselves whom thou hast called to thyself; and grant that every remembrance which turns our hearts from things seen to things unseen may lead us always upwards to thee, till we come to our eternal rest; through Jesus Christ our Lord.

Fenton John Anthony Hort, 1828–92, Bible scholar

Holding fast the Faith

291 A LMIGHTY God, in times of doubts and questionings, when our belief is perplexed by new learning, new teaching, new thought; when our faith is strained by creeds, by doctrines, by mysteries beyond our understanding, give us the faithfulness of learners and the courage of believers in thee.

Give us boldness to examine, and faith to trust all truth; patience and insight to master difficulties, stability to hold fast our traditions, to admit all fresh truth made known to us, and to combine it loyally and honestly with the old.

Save us and help us, we humbly beseech thee, O Lord.

George Ridding, 1828–1905, Bishop of Southwell

The thirst for souls

O BLESSED Jesus, our Lord and our Master, who wast pleased to thirst for our souls on the cross: grant that we may not be satisfied with the pleasures of this lower life, but ever thirst for the souls thou didst die to save, and, above all, to thirst for thee; for thine own Name's sake.

292

Edward King, 1829–1910, Bishop of Lincoln

The Light of the world

H EAVENLY Father, who didst give thy blessed Son to be the Light of the world, send out the knowledge of thy Word to all lands, and hasten thy kingdom. Shine with the fullness of thy truth and grace upon the whole Church; scatter the darkness of ignorance and error; knit all hearts unto thee and to one another; and finally bring us all to the light of everlasting life.

293

Lawrence Rayner Tuttiett, 1825–97, Canon of Perth Cathedral

Sufferers

294 ALMIGHTY and most merciful Father, who hast taught us not to think of ourselves only, but also of the wants of others, we remember before thee all who are burdened and oppressed, those whose hopes have been crushed and whose purposes are overthrown.

We remember also those who are afflicted by poverty, or worn down by sickness and disease, those who are in darkness or despair, or who are suffering for righteousness' sake.

Help them all, O God, to rest in thee for comfort and strength; through Jesus Christ our Lord.

Professor William Angus Knight, 1836–1916

Jealousy

295 O GOD, who givest to thy children liberally, preserve us from all envy at the good of our neighbour, and from every form of jealousy.

Teach us to rejoice in what others have and we have not, to delight in what they achieve and we cannot accomplish, to be glad in all that they enjoy and we do not partake of; and so fill us daily more completely with love, through our Saviour Jesus Christ.

Professor Knight

Dependence on God

O GOD, of whom and through whom and unto whom are all things, I acknowledge my utter dependence upon thee. I have nothing that I have not received. By thee I am sustained, in nature and grace, day by day, and moment by moment. Suffer not the work of thy hands to perish. Let thy Spirit empty me of all that is not thine, that Christ may dwell in me, and I in him.

Professor W. Gray Elmslie, 1848–89, Church of Scotland minister

296

Creator and Redeemer

ALMIGHTY God, who hast created man in thine own image, and made him a living soul that he might seek after thee and have dominion over thy creatures, teach us to study the works of thy hands that we may subdue the earth to our use, and strengthen our reason for thy service; and so to receive thy blessed word that we may believe on him whom thou hast sent to give us the knowledge of salvation and the remission of our sins. All which we ask in the name of the same Jesus Christ our Lord.

James Clark Maxwell, 1831–79, Scottish scientist

297

PRAYERS OF THE POETS
of the period
The singing heart

298   Lord, make my heart a place where angels sing!
     For surely thoughts low-breathed by thee
Are angels gliding near on noiseless wing;
     And where a home they see
Swept clean, and garnished with adoring joy,
     They enter in and dwell, and teach that heart to
       swell
With heavenly melody, their own untired employ.

John Keble, 1792–1866

The soul before God

299   Take me away, and in the lowest deep
     There let me be,
And there in hope the lone night-watches keep,
     Told out for me.
There, motionless and happy in my pain,
     Lone, not forlorn,
There will I sing my sad perpetual strain,
     Until the morn.
There will I sing, and soothe my stricken breast,
     Which ne'er can cease
To throb and pine, and languish, till possest
     Of its Sole Peace.

There will I sing my absent Lord and Love:
   Take me away,
That sooner I may rise, and go above,
And see him in the truth of everlasting day.

John Henry Newman, 1801–90, Cardinal, from
'The Dream of Gerontius'

Strong Son of God

STRONG Son of God, immortal Love,   300
   Whom we, that have not seen thy face,
  By faith, and faith alone, embrace,
Believing where we cannot prove.

Thou wilt not leave us in the dust;
   Thou madest man, he knows not why;
  He thinks he was not made to die,
And thou hast made him, thou art just.

Thou seemest human and divine,
   The highest, holiest manhood thou;
  Our wills are ours, we know not how;
Our wills are ours, to make them thine.

Our little systems have their day;
   They have their day and cease to be:
  They are but broken lights of thee,
And thou, O Lord, art more than they.

Alfred, Lord Tennyson, 1809–92

The lowest place

301 GIVE me the lowest place: not that I dare
    Ask for that lowest place, but thou hast died
That I might live and share
    Thy glory by thy side.

Give me the lowest place: or if for me
    That lowest place too high, make one more low
Where I may sit and see
    My God and love thee so.

Christina Rossetti, 1830–94

None beside thee

302 NONE other Lamb, none other Name,
    None other hope in heaven or earth or sea,
None other hiding-place from guilt and shame,
    None beside thee.

My faith burns low, my hope burns low,
    Only my heart's desire cries out in me
By the deep thunder of its want and woe,
    Cries out to thee.

Lord, thou art life though I be dead,
    Love's fire thou art however cold I be;
Nor heaven have I, nor place to lay my head,
    Nor home, but thee.

Christina Rossetti

I asked for Peace

I ASKED for Peace: 303
   My sins arose,
    And bound me close,
I could not find release.

I asked for Truth:
   My doubts came in,
    And with their din
They wearied all my youth.

I asked for Love:
   My lovers failed,
    And griefs assailed
Around, beneath, above.

I asked for thee:
   And thou didst come
    To take me home
Within thy heart to be.

Digby Mackworth Holben, 1848–67

To the Blessed Virgin

BE thou then O thou dear   304
  Mother, my atmosphere;
My happier world, wherein
To wend and meet no sin;
Above me, round me lie
Fronting my forward eye
With sweet and scarless sky;
Stir in my ears, speak there
O God's love, O live air,

Of patience, penance, prayer;
Worldmothering air, air wild,
Wound with thee, in thee isled,
Fold home, fast fold thy child.

Gerard Manley Hopkins, 1844–89, Jesuit; priest and poet

Sacramental prayer

305 GODHEAD here in hiding, whom I do adore,
Masked by these bare shadows, shape and
nothing more,
See, Lord, at thy service low lies here a heart
Lost, all lost in wonder at the God thou art . . .

Jesu, whom I look at shrouded here below,
I beseech thee send me what I thirst for so:
Some day to gaze on thee face to face in light
And be blest for ever with thy glory's sight.

Tr Gerard Manley Hopkins

★　　★　　★

Saint George's Day

306 O LORD God of hosts, who didst give grace to thy
servant George to lay aside the fear of man and
to confess thee even unto death: grant that we, and
all our countrymen who bear office in the world,
may think lightly of place and honour, and seek
rather to please the Captain of our salvation who
hath chosen us to be his soldiers; to whom, with thee
and the Holy Ghost, be thanks and praise from all
the armies of thy saints, now for evermore.

John Wordsworth, 1843–1911, Bishop of Salisbury

Trinity Sunday

O LORD God Almighty, immortal, invisible, the   307
mysteries of whose being are unsearchable:
accept, we beseech thee, our praises for the revelation which thou hast made of thyself, Father, Son,
and Holy Ghost, three Persons and one God; and
mercifully grant that, ever holding fast this faith, we
may magnify thy glorious Name; who livest and
reignest, one God, world without end.

John Dowden, 1886–1910, Bishop of Edinburgh

Liberal giving

S TIR up, we beseech thee, O Lord, the wills of thy   308
faithful people, that they who have freely received of thy bounty, may of thy bounty freely give;
through Jesus Christ our Lord.

Bishop Dowden

Fire of love

O SPIRIT of the living God, who dwellest in us,   309
who art holy, who art good: come thou, and
fill the hearts of thy faithful people, and kindle
within them the fire of thy love; through Jesus
Christ our Lord.

Catholic Apostolic Church, 1861

A prayer for Christian mothers

310 O LORD, fill us with thy Holy Spirit, that we may firmly believe in Jesus Christ, and love him with all our hearts. Wash our souls in his precious blood. Make us to hate sin and to be holy in thought, word, and deed. Help us to be faithful wives and loving mothers. Bless us and all who belong to the Mothers' Union; unite us in love and prayer, and teach us to train our children for heaven. Pour out thy Holy Spirit on our husbands and children. Make our homes, homes of peace and love, and may we so live on earth, that we may live with thee for ever in heaven; for Jesus Christ's sake.

Mary Sumner, 1828–1921; founder of the Mothers' Union, members'
prayer of 1876

Invocation

311 O GOD the Holy Ghost, who hast called us to thy service: as thou hast begun thy work, so also continue and finish it in us. Save us from our besetting sins, from pride, and bitterness, and faintness of heart; from sloth and self-deceit, and the curse of an unsubdued will; and grant us to know and to follow, to do and to suffer thy will; who with the Father and the Son livest and reignest one God, for ever and ever.

Richard William Church, Dean of St Paul's 1815–90

Intercession for the Jews

LOOK down in compassion, O Lord Christ, upon   312
thine own people, the Jews, in all parts of the
world. Open their hearts to receive thee, their true
Messiah and Saviour. Forgive those who have
persecuted them. Help us to care for them, and ever
to pray for the peace of Jerusalem; for thy sake, who
art both the Light to lighten the Gentiles and also the
Glory of thy people Israel.

Albert Frederick Thornhill, nineteenth century

For labourers in Christ's vineyard

O HEAVENLY Father, Lord of the harvest, have   313
respect to these our prayers and send forth
labourers into thy harvest. Fit and prepare them by
thy grace for the work of their ministry. Give them
the spirit of power, and of love, and of a sound
mind. Strengthen them to endure hardness; and
grant that both by their life and doctrine they may
set forth thy glory, and set forward the salvation of
all men; through Jesus Christ our Lord.

Church of Ireland Prayer Book, 1878

Harvest Thanksgiving

O ALMIGHTY God and Heavenly Father, we   314
glorify thee that thou hast again fulfilled to us
thy gracious promise, that while the earth re-
maineth, seedtime and harvest shall not fail. We

bless thee for the kindly fruits of the earth, which thou hast given for our use. Teach us to remember that it is not by bread alone that man doth live, and grant us evermore to feed on him who is the true bread from heaven, even Jesus Christ our Lord; to whom with thee and the Holy Ghost be all honour and glory, world without end.

Church of Ireland Prayer Book, 1878

For prison governors and warders

315 O HOLY Spirit of God, inspire with thy wisdom and love those set in chief authority over prisoners. Teach them to rule with mercy and with justice, neither despising nor neglecting their brethren whom thou hast put under their care; that they may show forth the spirit in which thou dost rule and judge the hearts of men; through Jesus Christ our Lord.

Guild of Saints Paul and Silas, 1881

The family and household

316 A LMIGHTY God, who art the author of all good-ness, look in mercy upon this family and household, and bless all who belong to it, present or absent. Save and defend us in all dangers and adversities, give us all things needful for our souls and bodies, and bring us safely to thy heavenly kingdom; through Jesus Christ our Lord.

Family Prayers of the Church of Ireland, 1895

Our daily life

O LORD Jesus Christ, we beseech thee to assist us   317
with thy heavenly grace, that we may be
blessed in our work this day, and above all things
attain the knowledge of thee, whom to know is life
eternal; and that, according to thy most holy example, we may ever be found going about amongst our
fellow-men, doing good; for thy Name's sake.

Adapted from Family Prayers, 1895

The Christian student

G RANT me, Lord, in all my studies,   318
Through all volumes roaming where I list,
Whatsoever spacious distance
   Rises in simple grandeur through thought's mist,
Whatsoever land I find me,
   That, of right divine, to claim for Christ.

*William Alexander, Archbishop of Armagh and Primate of all
Ireland, 1824–1911*

For hospitals and their staffs

O LORD Jesus Christ, who went about doing   319
good and healing all manner of sickness: give
strength, wisdom and gentleness to all thy ministering servants, our physicians, surgeons and nurses;
that always bearing thy presence with them, they

may not only heal but bless, and shine as lamps of hope in the darkest hours of distress and fear; who livest and reignest with the Father and the Holy Ghost, ever one God world without end.

Church Missionary Society, 1899

PRAYERS OF BISHOP BROOKE FOSS WESTCOTT, 1825–1901

For peace of heart

320   O LORD God, in whom we live and move and have our being, open our eyes that we may behold thy fatherly presence ever with us. Draw our hearts to thee with the power of thy love. Teach us to be anxious for nothing, and when we have done what thou givest us to do, help us, O God our Saviour, to leave the issue to thy wisdom. Take from us all doubt and mistrust. Lift our hearts up to thee in heaven, and make us to know that all things are possible to us through thy Son our Redeemer.

Love for Christ

321   O GOD, the God of all goodness and of all grace, who art worthy of a greater love than we can either give or understand: fill our hearts, we beseech thee, with such love toward thee that nothing may seem too hard for us to do or to suffer in obedience

to thy will; and grant that loving thee, we may become daily more like thee, and finally obtain the crown of life which thou hast promised to those that love thee; through Jesus Christ our Lord.

A new order

BEHOLD, O God, our strivings after a truer and more abiding order. Grant us visions of the better things thou hast prepared for us. Scatter every excuse of frailty and unworthiness. Consecrate us all with a heavenly mission; open to us a clearer prospect of our work; and give us strength gladly to welcome and gratefully to fulfil it, in the power and for the sake of Jesus Christ our Saviour.

322

Class unity

O LORD God, who by thy providence hast ordered various ranks among men, draw them ever closer together by thy Holy Spirit.

323

Teach us to know that all differences of class are done away in Christ.

Take from us and from our countrymen all jealousy and discontent.

Unite us one to another by a common zeal for thy cause, and enable us by thy grace to offer unto thee the fruits of our service; through Jesus Christ our Lord.

Brotherly love

324 ALMIGHTY and most merciful God, who hast given us a new commandment that we should love one another, give us also grace to fulfil it. Make us gentle, courteous, and forbearing. Direct our lives so that we may look to the good of others in word and deed. Hallow all our friendships by the blessing of thy Spirit, for the sake of your Son Jesus Christ our Lord.

The God of Truth

325 WE beseech thee, O God, the God of Truth, that what we know not of things we ought to know, thou wilt teach us.

That what we know of Truth, thou wilt keep us therein.

That what we are mistaken in, as men must be, thou wilt correct.

That at whatsoever things we stumble, thou wilt yet establish us.

And from all things that are false, and from all knowledge that would be hurtful, thou wilt evermore defend us; through Jesus Christ our Lord.

NOTE *Brooke Foss Westcott was one of the foremost Bible scholars of his time. His last eleven years were spent as Bishop of Durham, where he made social problems and the lot of the miners his special concern.*

PART V

THE TWENTIETH
CENTURY

Sectional Prayers:

Prayers of the Proposed Prayer Book, 1928
War-time Prayers of 1914–18 and 1939–45
Prayers of Archbishop William Temple
Prayers of the Scottish Churches
Prayers of the Church of Ireland
Welsh Prayers of the Century

5
Prayers of the Twentieth Century

The British Empire

O GOD, who hast made us members of the British 326 Empire, and hast bound us together by one Queen and one Flag, may we ever live in the remembrance of our great responsibilities. Help us to seek to excel in the practice of faith, courage, duty, self-discipline, fair dealing, even justice, and true sympathy; that as loyal patriots and good citizens we may each individually aid in elevating the British character, and as a God-fearing and a God-loving people glorify thee, the King of kings and Lord of lords; through Jesus Christ thy Son.

The 12th Earl of Meath, 1841–1909, founder of the Empire Movement

The birth of a child

O LORD God, in whose hands are the issues of 327 life, we thank thee for thy gifts to us at this time. We thank thee for the life given, and the life preserved. And as thou hast knit together life and love in one fellowship, so we pray thee to grant that with this fresh gift of life to us, there may be given an increase of love one to another; through Jesus Christ our Lord.

William Boyd Carpenter, 1841–1918, Bishop of Ripon

Absent friends

328 O LORD of Love, who art not far from any of thy children, watch with thy care those who are far away from us. Be thou about their path; be thou within their hearts; be thou their defence upon thy right hand; and give them unfailing trust in thee. Let not distance break the bonds of love which bind them to us and to thee, but knit us closer in thy love; for the sake of Jesus Christ our Lord.

Bishop Carpenter

For all classes of men

329 WE pray thee, O Lord, for all orders and states of men in our country; for those who bear rule and office, for all who have voice in elections, for all whom thou hast entrusted with wealth, for the middle classes, and for the multitudes of the poor. Let thy good Spirit stir up men in ever greater numbers to seek their neighbours' good, and to do the will of God in truth and love, to thy glory and the blessing of our land; through Jesus Christ our Lord.

Handley C. G. Moule, 1841–1920, Bishop of Durham

Benediction

THE blessing of the Lord 330
rest and remain upon all his people,
in every land and of every tongue;
The Lord meet in mercy all who seek him;
The Lord comfort all who suffer and mourn;
The Lord hasten his coming,
and give us his people peace by all means.

Bishop Moule

Our daily work

GRACIOUS God, remember us in our work this 331
day. If it be thy will, give us a prosperous day.
May all our work be well done. May we turn
nothing out half done. May we glorify thee by
honest good work; for the sake of him who com-
pleted his work for us, even Jesus Christ our Lord.

John Henry Jowett, CH, 1841–1923

Counting our blessings

O GOD our Father, we would thank thee for all 332
the bright things of life. Help us to see them,
and to count them, and to remember them, that our
lives may flow in ceaseless praise; for the sake of
Jesus Christ our Lord.

J. H. Jowett

The nation

333 O LORD God Almighty, who hast made for thy glory all nations over the face of the earth, that they may do thee service in the joy of freedom: give to this people of England the passion for righteousness, and the strength of self-control; that they may exercise their liberty with a single desire to fulfil thy gracious will; through Jesus Christ, our Master, Redeemer, and King.

Henry Scott Holland, 1847–1918, Canon of St Paul's

For life abundant

334 O LORD Christ, who camest that we might have life, and have it more abundantly, come and break down all that hinders life. Come and give us wisdom and patience, courage and resolution to discover how thy goodwill may verify itself to all. Give us life that we may give out life. Give unity, give brotherhood, give peace, for thine own sake.

Canon Holland

The communion of saints

335 O THOU who art the God of all the generations of men, we thank thee for all who have walked humbly with thee, and especially those near to us and dear, in whose lives we have seen the vision of thy beauty. May we know that in the body or out of

the body they are with thee. Unite us still, God of our souls, in one household of faith and love, one family in heaven and on earth; through Jesus Christ our Lord.

John Hunter, 1849–1917, Minister of Trinity Church, Glasgow

Generosity

MAKE us ever eager, O Lord, to share the good things that thou dost give us. Grant us such a measure of thy Spirit that we may find more joy in giving than in getting. Make us ready to give cheerfully without grudging, secretly without praise, and in sincerity without looking for gratitude. For Jesus Christ's sake.

336

John Hunter

In time of war

O GOD, who art the Father of all, and who makest men to be of one mind in a house, we beseech thee at this time of strife and unrest, to grant to us, by the inspiration of thy Holy Spirit, a fuller realisation of our brotherhood, man with man in thee. Allay all anger and bitterness, and deepen in us a sense of truth and equity in our dealings one with another; for the sake of thy Son, our Lord Jesus Christ.

337

Randall T. Davidson, 1848–1930, Archbishop of Canterbury

For those in authority

338   O LORD God Almighty, guide, we pray thee, our Sovereign and all those to whom thou hast committed the government of our nation and empire; and grant to them at this time special gifts of wisdom and understanding, of counsel and strength; that upholding what is right, and following what is true, they may obey thy holy will and fulfil thy divine purpose; through Jesus Christ our Lord.

Archbishop Davidson

For peace among the nations

339   ALMIGHTY God, from whom all thoughts of truth and peace proceed, kindle, we pray thee, in the hearts of all men the true love of peace, and guide with thy pure and peaceable wisdom those who take counsel for the nations of the earth; that in tranquillity thy kingdom may go forward, till the earth be filled with the knowledge of thy love; through Jesus Christ our Lord.

Francis Paget, 1851–1911, Bishop of Oxford

For the Spirit of Christ

340   OUR Father in heaven, we pray thee to send into our hearts, and into the hearts of all men everywhere, the Spirit of our Lord Jesus Christ.

John Oxenham (William Arthur Dunkerley), 1852–1941

At a general election

O LORD, we beseech thee to govern the minds of all who are called at this time to choose faithful men and women to serve in the great Council of the nation; that they may exercise their choice as in thy sight, for the welfare of all our people; through Jesus Christ our Lord. 341

Charles Gore, 1853–1932, Bishop of Oxford

Bible study

A LMIGHTY and most merciful God, who hast given the Bible to be the revelation of thy great love to man, and of thy power and will to save him: grant that our study of it may not be made in vain by the callousness or carelessness of our hearts, but that by it we may be confirmed in penitence, lifted to hope, made strong for service, and, above all, filled with the true knowledge of thee and of thy Son Jesus Christ. 342

Sir George Adam Smith, 1858–1942, Bible scholar, Principal of Aberdeen University

The blind

O GOD, who art the Father of lights, and with whom there is no darkness at all: we thank thee for the good gift of sight which thou hast bestowed upon us, and we pray thee to fill us with thine own compassion for those who have it not. 343

Direct and prosper the efforts that are made for their welfare. Reveal to them by thy Spirit the things which eye hath not seen, and comfort them with the hope of the light everlasting, to which, of thy great mercy, we beseech thee to bring us all; through Jesus Christ our Saviour.

Arthur W. Robinson, 1856–1928, Canon of Canterbury

Guidance

344 O ETERNAL God, the fountain of all wisdom and the giver of all grace, who didst send thy Spirit to dwell with our fathers and to lead them into the way of truth: grant to us that in all our difficulties and dangers we also may be enabled, by the light and power of the same Spirit, to know thy mind and to do thy will, for the glory of thy Name and the benefit of thy Church; through Jesus Christ our Lord.

Canon Robinson

Seekers after truth

345 O LORD God, whom to know is the life and joy of thy creatures, we thank thee for the light which has been given to seekers in all ages, and most of all through him who is the fullest revelation of thyself.

Grant us to hold firmly and faithfully the truth that has been shown to those before us, and enable us to appropriate it afresh according to our opportunity and capacity. May we not be daunted and discouraged by the mysteries or the shadows that perplex us, but understand that these things are necessarily part of our training; and strengthen our faith and patience.

Canon Robinson

For serenity and happiness

GRANT unto us, O Lord, the royalty of inward happiness and the serenity which comes from living close to thee. Daily renew in us the sense of joy, and let thy eternal Spirit dwell in our souls and bodies, filling every corner of our lives with light and gladness; so that bearing about with us the infection of a good courage, we may meet all life's ills or accidents with gallant and high-hearted happiness, giving thee thanks always for all things.

346

Lucy Helen Muriel Soulsby, 1856–1927

Intercession

O LORD, thou lover of souls, we beseech thee to give courage to thy soldiers, wisdom to the perplexed, endurance to sufferers, fresh vigour and interest in life to those who have lost heart, a sense of thy presence to the lonely, comfort to the dying, and a clear vision of thy truth to those who are seeking thee; for the sake of Jesus Christ our Lord.

347

L. H. M. Soulsby

PRAYERS OF THE PROPOSED
PRAYER BOOK, 1928

Saints of the Church of England

348 WE beseech thee, O Lord, to multiply thy grace upon us who commemorate the saints of our nation; that, as we rejoice to be their fellow-citizens on earth, so we may have fellowship also with them in heaven; through Jesus Christ our Lord.

For missions

349 O GOD of all the nations of the earth, remember the multitudes of the heathen, who, though created in thine image, are ignorant of thy love; and, according to the propitiation of thy Son Jesus Christ, grant that by the prayers and labours of thy holy Church they may be delivered from all superstition and unbelief, and brought to worship thee; through him whom thou hast sent to be our salvation, the Resurrection and the Life of all the faithful, the same thy Son Jesus Christ our Lord.

For places of learning

350 VOUCHSAFE, O Lord, to prosper with they blessing the work of all universities, colleges and schools; that they who serve thee therein, as teachers or learners, may set thy holy will ever before them,

and be led to the knowledge of thy truth; that so both Church and Commonwealth may be bettered by their studies, and they themselves be made meet to be partakers of eternal life; through Jesus Christ our Lord.

For our industries

ALMIGHTY God, who by thy Son Jesus Christ hast sanctified labour to the welfare of mankind: prosper, we pray thee, the industries of this land and all those who are engaged therein; that, shielded in all their temptations and dangers, and receiving a due reward of their labours, they may praise thee by living according to the will of thy Son, Jesus Christ our Lord.

351

The departed

O FATHER of all, we pray to thee for those whom we love, but see no longer. Grant them thy peace; let light perpetual shine upon them; and in thy loving wisdom and almighty power work in them the good purpose of thy perfect will; through Jesus Christ our Lord.

352

Benediction

GO forth into the world in peace; be of good courage; hold fast that which is good; render to no man evil for evil; strengthen the fainthearted;

353

support the weak; help the afflicted; honour all men; love and serve the Lord, rejoicing in the power of the Holy Spirit.

And the blessing of God Almighty, the Father, the Son, and the Holy Ghost, be upon you, and remain with you for ever.

★   ★   ★

Administration of justice

354　O GOD, mighty and merciful, the judge of all men: grant to those who minister justice the spirit of wisdom and discernment; and that they may be strong and patient, upright and compassionate, fill them, we beseech thee, with the spirit of thy holy fear; through Jesus Christ our Lord.

J. Armitage Robinson, 1858–1933, Dean of Wells

In time of international strife

355　HAVE mercy, O God, on our distracted and suffering world, on the nations perplexed and divided. Give to us and to all people a new spirit of repentance and amendment; direct the counsels of all who are working for the removal of the causes of strife and for the promotion of goodwill; and hasten the coming of thy kingdom of peace and love; through Jesus Christ our Lord.

Charles F. d'Arcy, 1859–1938, Archbishop of Armagh

Service chaplains

REMEMBER, O Lord, all whom thou hast called to minister to the souls of those engaged in warfare. Give them grace to enlighten the ignorant, to strengthen the weak-hearted, to comfort those who suffer, and to speak peace to the dying. So grant that in all their ministrations, in all their life and conversation, they may shepherd the men and women committed to their care, and advance the honour of our Saviour and his kingdom; through the same Jesus Christ our Lord.

356

Bishop John Taylor Smith, 1860–1938, Chaplain-General to the Forces in World War I

Celebration of the saints of England

GOD, whom all the saints adore, assembled in thy glorious presence from all times and places of thy dominion, and who hast adorned our country with many splendid lamps of holiness: grant us worthily to celebrate the saints of England by following their footsteps throughout the world, whithersoever thou shalt send us; till all nations confess thy Name and all mankind know and fulfil its destiny in Christ; to whom with thee and the Holy Ghost be all honour and glory, world without end.

357

Dr Alexander Nairne, 1862–1936

Service

358 MY God, my heart is set on serving thee. To serve the world is hard, unsatisfying, but to serve thee is perfect joy and liberty.

Here would I consecrate to thee and to thy cause each faculty and power which thou hast given me: of intellect or learning, of heart or sympathy, of spiritual fervour, of influence or guidance.

All come from thee, all shall revert to thee: I have only the use of them and that I give to thee. Take all and use it for thy holy purposes, use me to thy glory.

Walter Frere, 1863–1938, Bishop of Truro

Personal prayer before ordination

359 O LOVE, I give myself to thee, thine ever, only thine, to be. This day I consecrate all that I have or hope to be to thy service.

O crucified Lord, forgive the sins of my past life: fold me in the embrace of thy all-prevailing sacrifice; purify me by thy passion.

Son of Man, hallow all my emotions and affections, and make them strong only for thy service.

Eternal Word, sanctify my thoughts; make them free with the freedom of thy Spirit.

Son of God, consecrate my will to thyself: unite it with thine.

King of glory, my Lord and Master, take my whole being: use it in thy service, and draw it ever closer to thyself.

Cosmo Gordon Lang, 1864–1945, Archbishop of Canterbury, from a prayer written on the eve of his ordination as deacon, 1890

Music

O GOD, who in the gift of music hast given unto us a revelation of thy divine beauty: teach us to love thee in all thy gifts, and so devote ourselves in all our works to thy glory, that through music we may raise men from the sorrows of the world to the enjoyment of thy divine loveliness.

360

Harold Anson, 1867–1954, Master of the Temple

For agriculture

GIVE, O Lord, to all who till the ground the wisdom to understand thy laws, and to co-operate with thy wise ordering of the world. Give to men of science the power to discover the secrets of nature. Give to our statesmen the will to make just laws. Give to farmers and labourers the desire to work together in the spirit of justice and goodwill.

361

And grant that the fruits of thy bountiful earth may not be hoarded by selfish men or squandered by foolish men, but that all who work may share abundantly in the harvest of thy soil, according to thy will, revealed to us in Jesus Christ our Lord.

Harold Anson

The Church

362 O LORD, we beseech thee to maintain thy Church in truth and patience; that her pastors may be faithful, her watchmen vigilant, her flock loyal, her camp united, her warfare spiritual, her weapons heavenly, her lamp burning and shining; and as thy Son Jesus Christ hath given so great a price for us, let us not count it a hard thing to give up all for him, and to spend and be spent for the souls he hath redeemed; who liveth and reigneth with thee and the Holy Ghost, now and for evermore.

Percy Dearmer, 1867–1936, Canon of Westminster

The kingdom of God

363 O LORD, who hast set before us the great hope that thy kingdom shall come, and hast taught us to pray for its coming: give us grace to discern the signs of its dawning, and to work for the perfect day when thy will shall be done on earth as it is in heaven; through Jesus Christ our Lord.

Canon Dearmer

Missions

364 REMEMBER for good, we beseech thee, O Lord, the missionary work of thy Church in every land. Protect and provide for thy servants in the mission fields, and preserve them in every danger

and in all their needs; and give to the churches abroad and to us at home such an increased spirit of faith, sacrifice, and service that thy work may not be hindered but rather advanced, so that thy kingdom may come and the power of evil be driven back and overthrown; through Jesus Christ our Lord.

G. C. B. Bardsley, 1870–1940, Bishop of Leicester

Atomic power

ALMIGHTY and merciful God, without whom all things hasten to destruction and fall into nothingness: look, we beseech thee, upon thy family of nations and men, to which thou hast committed power in trust for their mutual health and comfort.

365

Save us and help us, O Lord, lest we abuse thy gift and make it our misery and ruin. Draw all men unto thee in thy kingdom of righteousness and truth, and renew our faith in thine unchanging purpose of goodwill and peace on earth; for the love of Jesus Christ our Lord.

Frederick B. Macnutt, 1873–1949, Provost of Leicester

For national unity

O LORD Jesus Christ, look in mercy, we beseech thee, upon this nation. Send out thy light and thy truth that they may lead us into paths of fellowship and peace. Break down all barriers of

366

contention and strife; and grant that seeking first thy kingdom and righteousness, we may live in brotherly unity and concord, to thy glory and the welfare of this realm.

Frank T. Woods, 1874–1932, Bishop of Winchester

For the nation

367

O GOD of earth and altar,
　　Bow down and hear our cry;
Our earthly rulers falter,
　　Our people drift and die;
The walls of gold entomb us,
　　The swords of scorn divide,
Take not thy thunder from us,
　　But take away our pride.

From all that terror teaches,
　　From lies of tongue and pen,
From all the easy speeches
　　That comfort cruel men,
From sale and profanation
　　Of honour and the sword,
From sleep and from damnation,
　　Deliver us, good Lord!

G. K. Chesterton, 1874–1936

The Commonwealth

368

ALMIGHTY God, Father of all men, under whose providence we are become members of a great Commonwealth of nations, and have in our keeping the government and protection of many peoples: give us such a spirit of wisdom and understanding, of justice and truth, of knowledge and of the fear of the Lord, that together we may ever abide in one bond of fellowship and service; to the glory of thy Name.

George W. Briggs, 1875–1959, Canon of Worcester

The perils of abundance

O GOD, who in thy love hast bestowed upon us gifts such as our fathers never knew nor dreamed of: mercifully grant that we be not so occupied with material things that we forget the things which are spiritual; lest, having gained the whole world, we lose our own soul; for thy mercy's sake.

369

Canon Briggs

Peace

A LMIGHTY God, whose kingdom alone bringeth true peace to the earth: reveal again thy law, that all nations may bow before it, and thine everlasting love, that they may dwell together in unity; through Jesus Christ our Lord.

370

After Cyril Garbett, 1875–1955, Archbishop of York

Christ our Saviour

371 O BLESSED Jesu Christ, who didst bid all who carry heavy burdens to come to thee, refresh us with thy presence and thy power. Quiet our understandings and give ease to our hearts, by bringing us close to things infinite and eternal. Open to us the mind of God, that in his light we may see light. And crown thy choice of us to be thy servants by making us springs of strength and joy to all whom we serve.

Evelyn Underhill, 1875–1941

For the new year

372 E TERNAL God, who makest all things new, and abidest for ever the same: grant us to begin this year in thy faith, and to continue it in thy favour; that, being guided in all our doings, and guarded all our days, we may spend our lives in thy service, and finally by thy grace attain the glory of everlasting life; through Jesus Christ our Lord.

William E. Orchard, 1877–1955, Minister of King's Weigh House Chapel, London

For world missions

373 O THOU, who art the light of the world, the desire of all nations, and the shepherd of our souls: let thy light shine in the darkness, that all the ends of the earth may see the salvation of our God.

By the lifting up of thy cross gather the peoples to thine obedience; let thy sheep hear thy voice, and be brought home to thy fold; so that there may be one flock, one shepherd, one holy kingdom of righteousness and peace, one God and Father of all, above all, and in all, and through all.

W. E. Orchard

Sympathy

GRANT us grace, O Father, not to pass by suffering or joy without eyes to see. Give us understanding and sympathy, and guard us from selfishness, that we may enter into the joys and sufferings of others. Use us to gladden and strengthen those who are weak and suffering; that by our lives we may help others to believe and serve thee, and shed forth thy light which is the light of life.

374

H. R. L. (Dick) Sheppard, 1880–1937, one time Vicar of St Martin-in-the Fields, later Dean of Canterbury

Petition

PEACE does not mean the end of all our striving; Joy does not mean the drying of our tears.
Give me, for light, the sunshine of thy sorrow,
Give me, for shelter, shadow of thy cross.
Give me to share the glory of thy morrow,
Gone from my heart the bitterness of loss.

375

G. A. Studdert Kennedy, 1883–1929, Army Chaplain, World War I

WAR-TIME PRAYERS OF 1914–18 AND 1939–45

At the outbreak of war

376 O GOD, who hast taught us in thy holy Word that thou dost not willingly afflict the children of men: grant that in the present time of warfare and distress of nations our people may know thy presence and obey thy will. Remove from us arrogance and feebleness; give us courage and loyalty, tranquillity and self-control, that we may accomplish that which thou givest us to do, and endure that which thou givest us to bear; for his sake who was lifted up on the cross to draw all men unto him, Jesus Christ our Lord.

A Form of Prayer, August 1914

In time of war

377 GOD of our fathers, on whom our confidence is set, who hast delivered us from of old, and wilt still deliver: support with thy whole might this people in the day of their proving; that they fear not the threatenings and strokes of the enemy, but stand to maintain thy cause, in the faith of thy Son, our Saviour Jesus Christ.

A Form of Prayer, March 1941

For those on active service

O ALMIGHTY Lord God, the Father and Protector
of all that trust in thee: we commend to thy
fatherly goodness the men and women who
through perils of war are serving this nation by land
or sea or in the air; beseeching thee to take into thine
own hand both them and the cause they serve.

Be thou their strength when they are set in the
midst of so many and great dangers; and make all
bold through death or life to put their trust in thee,
who art the only giver of victory and canst save by
many or by few; through Jesus Christ our Lord.

A Form of Prayer, October 1939

378

For prisoners of war

O MERCIFUL Father, look with thy tender compassion upon all prisoners of war. Supply all
their needs, and hasten the time of their release. Let
thy love protect them and thy presence cheer them;
that day by day in weariness and hardship they may
have strength to endure patiently, and may find
peace in thee; through Jesus Christ our Lord.

A Form of Prayer, August 1918

379

For our enemies

380 LORD Jesus Christ, before whose judgment seat we all shall stand, we pray as thou hast taught us for our enemies; so turn their hearts to thee that they may truly repent; and grant that they and we and all the peoples of the earth, being cleansed from sin, may know and do thy will, who wast lifted up upon the cross to draw all men to thyself, our Saviour, our Lord, and our God.

Form of National Prayer, 1942

For a righteous peace

381 O ALMIGHTY God, who canst bring good out of evil, and makest even the wrath of man turn to thy praise; we beseech thee so to order and dispose the issue of this war that we may be brought through strife to lasting peace; and that the nations of the world may be united in a new fellowship for the promotion of thy glory and the good of all mankind; through Jesus Christ our Lord.

Form of National Prayer, May 1940

★　★　★

Racial co-operation

382 LOVING Father, who hast made all men in thy likeness, and lovest all whom thou hast made: suffer not the world to separate itself from thee by building barriers of race and colour.

As thy Son our Saviour was born of a Hebrew mother yet rejoiced in the faith of a Syrian woman and a Roman soldier, welcomed the Greeks who sought him and suffered a man from Africa to carry his cross, so teach us rightly to regard the members of all races as fellow-heirs of thy kingdom; through the same Jesus Christ our Lord.

Toc H Prayers

Master Carpenter

JESUS, Master Carpenter of Nazereth, who on the cross through wood and nails didst work man's whole salvation: wield well thy tools in this thy workshop; that we who come to thee rough hewn, may by thy hand be fashioned to a truer beauty and a greater usefulness, for the honour of thy name.

383

Toc H Prayers

The unemployed

O LORD and heavenly Father, we commend to thy care the men and women of this land who are suffering distress and anxiety through lack of work. Strengthen and support them, we beseech thee; and so prosper the counsels of those who direct our industries that people may be set free from want and fear, to work in peace and security for the relief of their necessities and the well-being of the nation; through Jesus Christ our Lord.

384

Industrial Christian Fellowship, founded 1918

Welsh National Eisteddfod

385 GIVE us, Lord, your patronage,
And with patronage, give strength,
And in strength, understanding,
And in understanding, knowledge,
And in knowledge, knowledge of the Just,
And in knowledge of the Just, a love of the Just,
And in love, love of all that exists,
And in all that is, to love God,
God and all his goodness.

Prayer of Bardic Institution

A family prayer

386 OUR God and Father, we bow before you because you are the mighty one, blessed in
yourself and sharing your blessedness with all who
open their hearts to you. You have given us a joyous home and a wealth of love.

We thank you for father and mother and all our
family. Bless them, and through your Spirit make
us a blessing to them. Free us from all selfishness and
pride, from worries and faithless fears, and may the
angel of the covenant go with us on our journey.

Dedicate us to each other anew in your holy
love, and lead us and our neighbours to give our
home to you, so that at the last you may give your
glorious home to us; for the sake of Jesus Christ our
Lord.

Adapted from a prayer of the Welsh Calvinistic Methodist Church, 1926

For the Welsh nation

ALMIGHTY God, the King of Nations, who chose   387
the children of Israel, though a small nation, for
a high purpose: grant us in Wales both to develop
the gifts of nature and of grace with which you have
endowed us, and to be ready to share them with
others, while joyfully accepting what they have to
share with us; through your Son Jesus Christ our
Lord.

Welsh Book of Common Prayer, 1984

Church leaders in counsel

ETERNAL Father, who wouldst make the Church   388
of thy dear Son a city great and fair, the joy of
the whole earth: we beseech thee, by the sending of
thy Holy Spirit, to direct its counsels now in all
manner of wisdom, love, and might; remove per-
plexity, establish concord, kindle flame, and gather
a people single and strong in faith; to the praise of
him who with thee and the same Spirit liveth and
reigneth, one God, world without end.

Lambeth Conference, 1930

The spiritual needs of the nation

ALMIGHTY God, our heavenly Father, to forget   389
whom is to stumble and fall, to remember
whom is to rise again: we pray thee to draw the

people of this country to thyself. Prosper all efforts to make known to them thy truth, that many may learn their need of thee and thy love for them; so that thy Church and kingdom may be established among us to the glory of thy Name; through Jesus Christ our Lord.

Archbishop's Recall to Religion, 1937

Our responsibility

390   O LORD, who hast warned us that thou wilt require much of those to whom much is given: grant that we, whose lot is cast in so goodly a heritage, may strive together the more abundantly by all appointed means to extend to those who know thee not what we so richly enjoy; and as we have entered into the labours of others, so to labour that others may enter into ours, to the fulfilment of thy holy will; through Jesus Christ our Lord.

St Augustine's College, Canterbury

Travellers by road

391   ALMIGHTY God, giver of life and health, guide, we pray thee, with thy wisdom all who are striving to save from injury and death the travellers on our roads. Grant to those who drive along the highways consideration for others, and to those who walk on them or play beside them thoughtful caution and care; that so without fear or disaster we

all may come safely to our journey's end, by thy mercy who carest for us; through Jesus Christ our Lord.

Douglas Crick, Bishop of Chester, written for Road Safety Week, 1949

For enlightenment

O GOD, who clothest thyself with light as with a garment, and makest the outgoings of the morning and evening to praise thee: mercifully grant that, as by thy created light we perceive the wonders of thy universe, so by the uncreated light of thy Spirit we may discern the adorable majesty of thy being; and that, our hearts and minds being illumined by his presence, we may walk in thy paths without stumbling, until at last all shadows flee away, and in thy perfect light we see light; who with the Son and the Holy Spirit art God for evermore.

W. R. Matthews, 1881–1973, Dean of St Paul's

For the peace of the world

ETERNAL God, in whose perfect kingdom no sword is drawn but the sword of righteousness, and no strength known but the strength of love: we pray thee so mightily to shed and spread abroad thy Spirit, that all peoples and ranks may be gathered under one banner, of the Prince of Peace, as children of one God and Father of all; to whom be dominion and glory now and for ever.

Eric Milner-White, 1884–1964, Dean of York

The kingdom of God

394 O GOD and Father of all, whom the whole heavens adore: let the whole earth also worship thee, all kingdoms obey thee, all tongues confess and bless thee, and the sons of men love thee and serve thee in peace; through Jesus Christ our Lord.

Dean Milner-White

Commemoration of Holy Communion

395 WE adore thee, O God, and with our whole heart bless thee, who dost sustain and renew us with the communion of the most holy Body and Blood of our Saviour Jesus Christ, the utmost glory of thy love, the very seal of our redemption, the wonder of our souls; and we beseech thee that he may abide in us, speaking grace and peace to our lives, until we be possessed of everlasting life in him; to whom with thee and the Holy Ghost, one God, be glory and worship world without end.

Dean Milner-White

PRAYERS OF ARCHBISHOP WILLIAM TEMPLE, 1881–1944

For the nations

396 O ALMIGHTY God, the Father of all mankind, we pray thee to turn to thyself the hearts of all peoples and their rulers, that by the power of thy

Holy Spirit peace may be established among the nations on the foundation of justice, righteousness, and truth; through him who was lifted up on the cross to draw all men unto himself, even thy Son Jesus Christ our Lord.

For social justice

O ALMIGHTY God, who hast entrusted this earth unto the children of men, and through thy Son Jesus Christ hast called us unto a heavenly citizenship: grant us, we humbly beseech thee, such shame and repentance for the disorder and injustice and cruelty which are among us, that fleeing unto thee for pardon and for grace we may henceforth set ourselves to establish that city which has justice for its foundation and love for its law, whereof thou art the architect and maker; through the same Lord Jesus Christ, thy Son, our Saviour.

397

For industrial peace

O GOD, the King of righteousness, lead us, we pray thee, in ways of justice and peace; inspire us to break down all tyranny and oppression, to gain for every man his due reward, and from every man his due service; that each may live for all and all may care for each, in the name of Jesus Christ our Lord.

398

For the unity of the Church

399 O GOD, the physician of men and nations, the restorer of the years that have been destroyed: look upon the distractions of the world and the divisions of thy Church, and be pleased to stretch forth thy healing hand. Draw all men unto thee and one to another by the bands of thy love; make thy Church one, and fill it with thy Holy Spirit, that by thy power it may unite the world in a brotherhood of nations, wherein justice and mercy, truth and freedom, may flourish, and thou mayest be for ever glorified; through Jesus Christ our Lord.

Dedication

400 ALMIGHTY and eternal God, so draw our hearts to thee, so guide our minds, so fill our imaginations, so control our wills, that we may be wholly thine, utterly dedicated unto thee; and then use us, we pray thee, as thou wilt, but always to thy glory and the welfare of thy people; through our Lord and Saviour Jesus Christ.

Benediction

401 MAY the love of the Lord Jesus draw us to himself;
may the power of the Lord Jesus strengthen us in his service;
may the joy of the Lord Jesus fill our souls;

and may the blessing of God Almighty,
    the Father, the Son, and the Holy Ghost,
be with you and abide with you always.

NOTE *William Temple, the son of a previous Archbishop of Canterbury, was a churchman deeply involved in the social issues of the day and the cause of church unity. Archbishop of York for over twelve years, he was translated to Canterbury in 1942. His sudden death two years later robbed the nation of an outstanding spiritual leader.*

★   ★   ★

The church in the parishes

O LORD Jesus Christ, who didst go, as thy cus-   402
tom was, into the synagogue on the Sabbath
day: quicken with thy abiding presence the life of
thy Church in our parishes; that every church may
be as a city set on a hill, a witness to thy claims upon
our worship and service, a power-house of prayer,
and a joy and comfort to thy servants. Hear us from
thy throne in heaven, where with the Father and the
Holy Spirit thou livest and reignest, one God, world
without end.

Peter Green, 1871–1961, Canon of Manchester

The clergy as evangelists

M ERCIFUL and gracious Father, who wouldest   403
have all men to be saved and to come to the
knowledge of the truth: stir in the hearts of the
clergy a desire to do the work of an evangelist and to

make full proof of their ministry; that those who are as yet unconverted may hear thy summons to choose whom they will serve and may own thee Lord of all; for Jesus Christ's sake.

Canon Green

Family life

404 ALMIGHTY God and heavenly Father, whose Son Jesus Christ shared at Nazareth the life of an earthly home: send thy blessing, we beseech thee, upon all Christian families. Grant to parents the spirit of understanding and wisdom; give to the children the spirit of obedience and true reverence; and so bind each to each with the bond of mutual love, that every Christian family may be an image of the Holy Family, and every Christian home a school of heavenly knowledge and of virtuous living; through the same Jesus Christ our Lord.

Adapted from a prayer of Professor E. C. Ratcliff for the London diocese, 1948

For children in need

405 O GOD, the Father of all, we commend to your ceaseless compassion all homeless children and orphans, and those whose lives are overshadowed by violence, or thwarted by disease or cruelty. Awaken in us your living charity that we may not rest while children cry for bread, or go uncomforted for lack of love.

The Mothers' Union Service Book, 1980

World poverty and hunger

O GOD our Father, in the name of him who gave 406
bread to the hungry we remember all who
through our human ignorance, selfishness and sin
are condemned to live in want; and we pray that all
endeavours for the overcoming of world poverty
and hunger may be so prospered that there may be
found food sufficient for all; through Jesus Christ
our Lord.

Christian Aid

For compassion

O THOU whose divine tenderness ever outsoars 407
the narrow loves and charities of earth, grant
us a kind and gentle heart towards all that live. Let us
not ruthlessly hurt any creature of thine. Let us take
thought also for the welfare of little children, and of
those who are sick, and the poor; remembering that
what we do unto the least of these his brethren we do
unto Jesus Christ our Lord.

Professor John Baillie, 1886–1960, University of Edinburgh

Mental health

L ORD Jesus Christ, you healed many who were 408
mentally ill, and in your name we pray for a
deeper understanding of those whose minds are
disturbed. Give knowledge and skill to those who

treat them, patience and kindness to those who nurse them; and draw together in a closer fellowship of healing all who are working to further your will by making men whole.

Basil Naylor, Canon of Liverpool, in 'New Every Morning', 1973

People of other religions

409 ETERNAL God, Father of all mankind, you have shown yourself to the world in many ways, and have never left yourself without witness in the lives of men: hear our prayer for people whose faith and customs differ from ours. Make us ready to learn from them, and also eager to share with them the riches of your truth, which you have given us in Jesus Christ our Lord.

James M. Todd, Minister of the English Presbyterian Church, in 'New Every Morning', 1973

For the renewal of the Church

410 ALMIGHTY and everlasting God, who didst form thy Church to be of one heart and soul in the power of the resurrection and the fellowship of the Holy Spirit: renew her evermore in her first love; and grant to thy people such a measure of thy grace that their life may be hallowed, their way directed, and their work made fruitful to the good of thy Church and the glory of thy holy Name; through the same Jesus Christ our Lord.

Community of the Resurrection, founded 1892

An act of dedication

L ORD God, I am no longer my own, but thine. Put   411
me to what thou wilt, rank me with whom thou
wilt; put me to doing, put me to suffering; let me be
employed for thee, or laid aside for thee; exalted for
thee, or brought low for thee; let me be full, let me
be empty; let me have all things, let me have
nothing; I freely and heartily yield all things to thy
pleasure and disposal.

And now, O glorious and blessed God, Father,
Son, and Holy Spirit, thou art mine, and I am thine.
So be it. And the covenant which I have made on
earth let it be ratified in heaven.

Methodist Covenant Service

Christmas light and peace

O GOD our Father, who by the glorious birth of   412
thy Son didst enlighten the darkness of the
world, we pray that the light of his presence may
shine more and more in the lives of men; that, being
filled with his spirit of goodwill, the nations may
inherit that gift of peace which he came to bring. We
ask it in his Name.

Hugh Martin, CH, 1890–1964, Baptist minister, scholar and author

The Blessed Virgin Mary

413   O GOD, our Father, through the Holy Spirit you prepared the body and soul of the glorious virgin mother, Mary, to be a fit dwelling-place for your Son. As we celebrate her memory with joy grant that through her motherly intercession we may be preserved from evil in this world and from eternal death. We make this prayer to you through your Son Jesus Christ, who lives and reigns with you for ever and ever.

Catholic Prayer Book, 1970

Our Christian life

414   O GOD, our Father, direct and control us in every part of our life:
our tongues, that we speak no false words;
our actions, that we may do nothing to shame ourselves or hurt others;
our minds, that we may think no evil or bitter thoughts:
our hearts, that they may be set only on pleasing you;
through Jesus Christ our Lord.

Catholic Prayer Book, 1970

Prayer for unity

415   O GOD, our Father,
you are the God of all men equally:
Father of those who believe in you,

and equally of those who don't.
Send your Holy Spirit, the Spirit who unites
    people,
so that all men will forget their differences,
put aside their prejudices,
and work together for the good of all.
Unite especially those who believe in your Son,
all Christians, Catholic, Orthodox and Protestant
(and all those in between).
Break down the divisions between Christians
so that soon all may be united again
and once more be one family around your table.

Adapted and shortened from Catholic Prayer Book, 1970

In troubled Northern Ireland

LORD Jesus Christ, you are the way of peace.   416
  Come into the brokenness of this land with
    your healing love.
Help us to be willing to bow before you in true
    repentance,
and to bow to one another in real forgiveness.
By the fire of the Holy Spirit melt our hard hearts
and consume the pride and prejudice
which separate us from each other.
Fill us, O Lord, with your perfect love which casts
    out fear,
and bind us together in that unity which you share
with the Father and the Holy Spirit for ever.

Cecil Kerr, Rostrevor Reconciliation Centre

417   LORD Jesus Christ, by your cross and Passion humble our hearts to express a true repentance for all our sins.

We pray that the reconciling power of your cross may become more and more evident among us.

May your victory over the powers of evil in your resurrection from the dead give us courage and hope to work for a true and lasting peace in our land; for your Name's sake.

Prayer used in the churches of Northern Ireland, Easter 1978

418   HEAR our prayers, O Lord, for all who have died, or been maimed or injured through acts of violence.

We pray too for those who mourn their dead and for those who care for the injured.

Grant, Lord, that those caught up in the spiral of violence may turn from this dreadful evil, and that your peace may come to all the people of Ireland.

United Service for Peace, Cork, March 1989

Reconciliation

419   LORD Christ, who by your cross and resurrection reconciled the world to God
and broke down the barriers of class and colour
   which divide people and nations:
make us all instruments of reconciliation
   in the life of our world,

that we may inherit the blessing
   which you promised to the peacemakers.

'New Every Morning', 1973

Prayer for conversion of heart

ALMIGHTY and merciful God,
open my eyes to see the evil I have done.
Wherein sin has separated me from you,
may your love unite me to you again;
where sin has brought weakness,
may your power heal and strengthen;
where sin has brought death,
may your Spirit raise to new life.
Give me a new heart to love you,
so that my life may reflect the image of your Son.

420

Holy Year Prayer Book, 1983

In Christ's service

JESUS, Lord and Master, teach us and all your
people so to follow the pattern of your manhood
that we may learn to interpret life in terms of giving,
not of getting; to be faithful stewards of our time
and talents and of all you have entrusted to us; and to
buy up every opportunity of serving the needs of
others and advancing your kingdom in the world; to
the glory of your name.

421

F.C. in 'New Every Morning', 1973

Sufferers from nervous illness

422 LORD of great compassion, we pray you for those
who are nervously ill, and too weak and anxious
to lift themselves above the fear and sadness that
threatens to overwhelm them.

Do you yourself, O Lord, lift them up and
deliver them, as you delivered your disciples in the
storm at sea, strengthening their faith and banishing
their fear.

Turning to you, O Lord, may they find you, and
finding you may they find also all you have laid up
for them within the fortress of your love.

Elizabeth Goudge, 1900–84

A prayer of dedication

423 ALMIGHTY God,
we thank you for the gift of your holy word.
May it be a lantern to our feet,
a light to our paths,
and a strength to our lives.
Take us and use us
to love and serve all men
in the power of the Holy Spirit
and in the name of your Son,
Jesus Christ our Lord.

C. of E. Alternative Service Book, 1980

The caring Church

Most merciful Father, you have called us to be a 424
caring Church, reflecting in our lives your
infinite care for us your children.

Help us to fulfil our calling and to care for one
another in an unselfish fellowship of love; and to
care for the world around us in sharing with it the
good news of your love and serving those who
suffer from povery, hunger and disease.

We ask it in the name of Christ our Lord.

Michael Ramsey, 1904–88, Archbishop of Canterbury

For a just social order

O GOD, whose Son Jesus Christ cared for the 425
welfare of everyone and went about doing
good to all: grant us the imagination and resolution
to create in this country and throughout the world a
just social order for the family of man; and make us
agents of your compassion to the suffering, the
persecuted and the oppressed, through the Spirit of
your Son who shared the sufferings of men, our
pattern and our redeemer, Jesus Christ.

Norwich Cathedral, 1975

The sanctity of life

426 LORD God Almighty, our Creator, teach us to understand more and more profoundly that every human life is sacred, whether it belongs to an unborn infant or to a terminally-ill patient, to a handicapped child or to a disabled adult.

Remind us, heavenly Father, that each individual has been made in your image and likeness and has been redeemed by Christ.

Help us to see each other with your eyes, so that we may reverence, preserve and sustain your gift of life in them, and use our own lives more faithfully in your service.

We ask this through Christ our Lord.

Basil Hume OSB, b. 1. 9, Cardinal Archbishop of Westminster

The meaning of love

427 LORD Jesus, you have taught us that love is the fulfilling of the law.

Teach us now what love really is, how much it costs, how far it leads, how deep it digs into our selfish lives.

Then give us the courage and the generosity to accept what this means today and tomorrow and in the whole future way of our lives.

Fr Michael Hollings, b. 1921

For love and understanding

GOD of mercy and love, fill my heart anew
with your divine love. 428

Fill my thinking with your touchstone of grace
and understanding.

Guide my judgment of others made in your
image.

Help me to be your instrument of
reconciliation.

Help me to overcome human reaction to people
and events with something of your love for
others.

Forgive me when I doubt your power to heal
relationships and make all things new.

Robert H. A. Eames, b. 1937, Archbishop of Armagh

For peace

O GOD of many names,
Lover of all nations, 429

We pray for peace
in our hearts,
in our homes,
in our nations,
in our world,
the peace of your will,
the peace of our need.

Bishop George Appleton, b. 1902

Gloria

430 GLORY to you, O God, Creator and Father,
for the universe in which we live,
and for men made in your own image.
Glory to you, O Christ,
who took a human body
and redeemed our fallen nature.
Glory to you, O Holy Spirit,
who made our bodies
the temples of your presence.
Glory to Father, Son, and Holy Spirit,
whose will it is that we should be made whole
in body, mind and spirit.
Glory to God to all eternity.

Bishop Appleton

PRAYERS OF THE SCOTTISH CHURCHES

The Church of Scotland: Book of Common Order

The Lord's Supper

431 MOST gracious Father, who callest us to the Holy Table of our Saviour, to show his death and to receive his gift of life: enable us to come with earnest faith and kindled devotion. Help us to make the memorial of our Saviour's sacrifice with adoration and praise. Open our eyes to behold the vision of his love, and pour into our souls the fullness of his grace. And grant that, yielding ourselves to thee, we may henceforth live as those who are not their own,

but are bought with a price; through Jesus Christ our Lord, to whom with thee and the Holy Spirit be all honour and glory, world without end.

The communion of saints

REJOICING in the communion of saints, we remember with thanksgiving before thee, O Lord, all thy faithful servants, and those dear to us, who are at rest in thee . . . Keep us in unbroken fellowship with thy whole Church in heaven and on earth, and grant us at last to rejoice together in thine eternal kingdom; through Jesus Christ our Lord, who liveth and reigneth, and is worshipped and glorified with thee, O Father, and the Holy Spirit, world without end.

432

For human brotherhood

O GOD our Father, increase in every nation the sense of human brotherhood, true respect for man and for woman, loyalty in service and charity, happiness in work, and justice in reward; that our homes may be kept safe and pure, our cities renewed in beauty and order, and all the world may reflect the radiance of thy kingdom; through Jesus Christ our Lord.

433

For arts and letters

434   O GOD, who by thy Spirit in our hearts dost lead men to desire thy perfection, to seek for truth, and to rejoice in beauty: illumine, we pray thee, and inspire all thinkers, writers, artists, and craftsmen; that in whatsoever is true and pure and lovely, thy name may be hallowed and thy kingdom come on earth; through Jesus Christ our Lord.

435   DIRECT and bless, we beseech thee, O Lord, those who in this our generation speak where many listen, and write what many read; that they may do their part in making the heart of the people wise, its mind sound, and its will righteous; to the honour of Jesus Christ our Lord.

Scottish Episcopal Church: Book of Common Prayer

Saint Margaret of Scotland

436   O GOD, who didst call thy servant Queen Margaret to an earthly throne that she might advance thy heavenly kingdom, and didst endue her with zeal for thy Church and charity towards thy people: mercifully grant that we who commemorate her example may be fruitful in good works, and attain to the glorious fellowship of thy saints; through Jesus Christ our Lord.

(Feast day, November 16)

Pentecost

O ALMIGHTY God, who on the day of Pentecost 437
didst send the Holy Ghost, the Comforter, to
abide in thy Church unto the end of time: bestow
upon us, and upon all thy faithful people, his mani-
fold gifts of grace; that, with minds enlightened by
his truth and hearts purified by his presence, we may
day by day be strengthened with power in the
inward man; through Jesus Christ our Lord, who
with thee and the same Spirit liveth and reigneth one
God, world without end.

The judgment-seat of Christ

O LORD Jesus Christ, before whose judgment- 438
seat we must all appear and give account of the
things done in the body: grant, we beseech thee, that
when the books are opened in that day, the faces of
thy servants may not be ashamed; through thy
merits, O Blessed Saviour, who livest and reignest
with the Father and the Holy Spirit, one God, world
without end.

Epiphany

A LMIGHTY God, who at the baptism of thy 439
blessed Son Jesus Christ in the river Jordan
didst manifest his glorious Godhead: grant, we
beseech thee, that the brightness of his presence may
shine in our hearts, and his glory be set forth in our
lives; through the same Jesus Christ our Lord.

For a blessing on fisheries

440 O ALMIGHTY God, who madest the sea, and gavest all that moveth therein for the use of man: bestow thy blessing, we beseech thee, on the harvest of the waters that it may be abundant in its season; protect from every peril of the deep all fishermen and mariners, and grant that they may with thankful hearts acknowledge thee, who art the Lord of the sea and of the dry land; through Jesus Christ our Lord.

PRAYERS OF THE CHURCH OF IRELAND

Saint Patrick

441 O ALMIGHTY God, who in thy providence didst choose thy servant Patrick to be the apostle of the Irish people, that he might bring those who were wandering in darkness and error to the true light and knowledge of thee: grant us so to walk in that light, that we may come at last to the light of everlasting life; through the merits of Jesus Christ thy Son our Lord.

A Christian society

442 LOOK, we beseech thee, O Lord, upon the people of this land who are called after thy holy Name; and grant that they may ever walk worthy of their

Christian profession. Grant unto us all that, laying aside our divisions, we may be united in heart and mind to bear the burdens which are laid upon us. Help us to respond to the call of our country according to our several powers; put far from us selfish indifference to the needs of others; and give us grace to fulfil our daily duties with sober diligence. Keep us from all uncharitableness in word or deed, and enable us by patient endurance in well-doing to glorify thy Name; through Jesus Christ our Lord.

Home missions

O LORD Jesus Christ, thou good Shepherd of the sheep, who didst come to seek and to save that which was lost: we beseech thee to be present in thy power with the missions of thy Church in this our land. Show forth thy compassion to the helpless, enlighten the ignorant, succour those in peril, and bring home the wanderers in safety to thy fold; who livest and reignest with the Father and the Holy Spirit, one God world without end.

443

For broken homes

O LORD Jesus Christ, Son of a Virgin, born in a stable, and carried in infant weakness into exile: have mercy on all children who lack settled homes and dwelling places, and grant that those whose families are divided by sin or separated by law may be united in the family of thy Church, and

444

brought at last to that home where with the Father and the Holy Spirit thou livest and reignest, ever one God, world without end.

For peace with one another

445   O GOD, the Father of all mankind, we beseech thee to inspire us with such love, truth and equity, that in all our dealings with one another we may show forth our brotherhood in thee; for the sake of Jesus Christ our Lord.

For inner peace

446   O HEAVENLY Father, in whom we live and move and have our being, we humbly pray thee so to guide and govern us by thy Holy Spirit, that in all the cares and occupations of our daily life we may never forget thee, but remember that we are ever walking in thy sight; through Jesus Christ our Lord.

Thanksgiving for God's gifts

447   O GOD of love, we yield thee thanks for whatsoever thou hast given us richly to enjoy, for health and vigour, for the love and care of home, for the joys of friendship, and for every good gift of happiness and strength. We praise thee for all thy servants who by their example and encouragement

have helped us on our way, and for every vision of thyself which thou hast given us in sacrament or prayer; and we humbly beseech thee that all these thy benefits we may use in thy service and to the glory of thy holy Name; through Jesus Christ thy Son our Lord.

WELSH PRAYERS OF THE CENTURY

For the Church

SAVE your Church, O Lord, from the fear of the truth, so that it may not be found to strive against you under the cloak of zeal.

448

Make it ready to serve you along new paths when called to do so; and grant that its knowledge of you be so strong and living that it is compelled to sing to the Lord a new song.

In all difficulties and troubles intensify in it that love which hopes all things, endures all things, and which never behaves itself unseemly, but is always willing to be of help.

Herbert Morgan, 1875–1946, University of Wales

Supplication to the Trinity

449 HELP me at all times, O God, to encourage and not to dishearten, to be more ready to praise than to condemn, to uplift rather than to disparage, to hide rather than to expose the faults of others.

O risen and exalted Christ, dwell in me, that I may live with the light of hope in my eyes, the Word of life on my lips, and your love in my heart.

Help me, O Holy Spirit, to seek you faithfully, to hold you steadfastly, to show you unfailingly, for Christ's sake.

T. Glyn Thomas, 1905–73, Tr. W. Rhys Nicholas, b. 1914

Freedom from fear

450 GRACIOUS Lord, grant that we may know sufficient about ourselves to feel afraid, and know enough about you to lose our fears. At the height of our temptations may we be fortified by your strength. Although we may often lose heart, let us not forget the Intercessor with the Father, Jesus Christ the righteous.

Give us a keen intellect to recognise his voice in every difficulty, on the steep hills and in the deep valleys where the darkness gathers. Lead us to the light: you are the Light. We were not meant to walk in darkness nor to live in fear. Neither the number of sorrowful nights nor the depth of the gloom shall be too much if in the end you bring us safely to the full noon of your love.

H. Elvet Lewis, 1860–1955, Welsh poet

Praise

THE miracle was yours, O Christ, Son of God: 451
you have given me zest for life. You possessed
me through your Holy Spirit, and while I live I
cannot but sing. Today I see the beauty that is
unblemished; I feel the thrill that awakens my soul.

You alone deserve the praise, O blameless One;
the true meaning of life is in you. The void is filled
by your Word, and the far-off comes nearer in you,
O Son of Mary. The melodies of creation are for
your sake, and I see your glory on every hill. The
hallelujah is in my soul, and to you, Lord Jesus, I
give my praise.

W. Rhys Nicholas

The Church in Wales

ALMIGHTY God, who by the power of thy Holy 452
Spirit sent forth thine apostles to make disciples
of all nations, and to baptise them into thy Church:
renew, we beseech thee, by the same Spirit the
Church in Wales, that with wisdom and fervent zeal
we may continue to proclaim thy gospel, till all are
brought into the clear light and true knowledge of
thee and of thy Son, Jesus Christ our Lord.

Church in Wales Book of Common Prayer, 1984

Creator Spirit

453
CREATOR Spirit, move in all our hearts,
giving us new insight into the mysteries of
God
and a new determination to live by the gospel,
so that we, with all humanity,
may find our unity in Christ.

Presbyterian Church of Wales, Prayer Handbook 1989

Acknowledgments

The editor and publisher express their thanks to the following for permission to reproduce copyright prayers in this anthology.

Oxford University Press for a prayer by John Baillie from *A Diary of Private Prayer*, 1948; and two prayers of George Briggs from *Daily Prayers*, 1946.

BBC Publications for prayers from *New Every Morning*, 1973.

A. R. Mowbray for prayers from *The Prayer Manual*, 1951, compiled by Frederick B. Macnutt, and for prayers of Eric Milner-White, *After the Third Collect*, 1952.

Catholic Truth Society for a prayer from *Holy Year Prayer Book*, 1973.

Darton, Longman & Todd for prayers from *Catholic Prayer Book*, 1970, edited by Anthony Bullen.

The Central Board of Finance of the Church of England for prayers from the Proposed Prayer Book, 1928, and a prayer from The Alternative Service Book, 1980.

The Committee on Public Worship of the Church of Scotland for prayers from the Book of Common Order, 1940.

The Publications Committee of the Scottish Episcopal Church for prayers from the Book of Common Prayer, 1912.

The Standing Committee of the General Synod of

the Church of Ireland for prayers from the Book of Common Prayer, 1960, and *Occasional Prayers*, 1970.

The Church in Wales Publications for two prayers from the Book of Common Prayer, 1984.

Cardinal Archbishop Basil Hume OSB.

Robert H. A. Eames, Archbishop of Armagh.

Bishop George Appleton.

Fr Michael Hollings.

Grateful acknowledgment is also made for the use of prayers by the Rev. Harold Anson, Bishop Douglas Crick, Canon Peter Green, Dean W. R. Matthews. Canon Basil Naylor, the Rev. James M. Todd, Dr Hugh Martin, CH, Bishop Michael Ramsey, Evelyn Underhill, Elizabeth Goudge; and prayers of the Mothers' Union, the Community of the Resurrection, the Industrial Christian Fellowship, Christian Aid, and Toc H.

The prayers of Archbishop William Temple are reproduced from *Parish Prayers* (Hodder & Stoughton 1967) where they were published with permission of Mrs Frances Temple.

Index of Sources

Accession Service, 212–13
Addison, L., 198
Alcuin of York, 13–15
Alexander, Abp W., 318
Alford, Henry, 248
Alfred, King, 18–19
Alternative Service Book, 423
Andrewes, Bp Lancelot, 132–7
Anne, Queen, 186
Anselm, St, 26–8
Anson, Harold, 360–1
Appleton, Bp George, 429–30
Arnold, Thomas, 252
Austen, Jane, 250

Bacon, Francis, Viscount St Albans, 182
Baillie, Prof John, 407
Baker, Sir Henry W., 282
Bardic Institution, Welsh, 385
Bardsley, Bp G. C. B., 364
Baxter, Richard, 172–3
Becon, T., 72
Bede, the Venerable, 8–10
Benson, Abp, Edward W., 271–2
Benson, Richard M., 285–6
Blomfield, Abp Charles J., 236
Bonar, Horatius, 281
Bonnell, James, 202–3
Book of Common Order, 431–5
Book of Common Prayer, 79–94,
    145–52
Book of Hours 1514, 58
Bradford, J., 65
Brevint, D., 170
Briggs, G. W., 368–9
Bright, William, 276–8
Brough, W., 175
Bull, Henry, 117
Burns, Robert, 230
Butler, W. J., 268
Byrne, Mary, tr, 16

Caedmon, 7
Campion, Thomas, 219
Canons of 1603, 126
Canute, King, 24
Carpenter, Bp W. Boyd, 327–8
Catholic Apostolic Church, 309
Catholic Prayer Book, 413–15

Celtic prayers (various), 38–55
Chalmers, Thomas, 231
Channing, W. E., 238
Charles I, King, 184–5
Chesterton, G. K., 367
Christian Aid, 406
Christian Prayers 1566, 109–10
Christian Prayers 1578, 117–18
Church Missionary Society, 319
Church of Ireland, 313–14, 316–17,
    441–7
Church of Scotland, 431–5
Church in Wales, 387, 452
Church, R. W., 311
Colet, John, 56
Colquhoun, F., 421
Columba, St, 4–6
Community of the Resurrection, 410
Cosin, Bp John, 148, 150, 153–5
Coverdale, Bp Miles, 73–4
Cowper, William, 229
Cranmer, Abp Thomas, 68–70
Crawshaw, Richard, 225
Crick, Bp D., 391
Cromwell, Oliver, 183
Cromwell, Thomas, 62

d'Arcy, Abp C. F., 355
Davidson, Abp Randall T., 337–8
Dawson, G., 273
Dearmer, Percy, 362–3
Dekker, T., 127
Doddridge, Philip, 210
Donne, John, 138, 220
Dowden, Bp John, 307–8
Drake, Sir Francis, 98
Dunstan, St, 22

Eames, Abp R. H. A., 428
Edelwald, Bp, 20
Edward VI, King, 63
Egbert, Abp, 11–12
Eliot, George, 257
Elizabeth, Queen, 96–7
Elmslie, Prof W. G., 296
Erigena, J. Scotus, 21
Ethelwold, Bp, 23
Evans, Christmas, 233–4
Evelyn, John, 195

Frere, Bp W., 358
Froude, R. H., 243
Fuller, Thomas, 157

Garbett, Abp Cyril, 370
Garter, Order of the, 32
Gladstone, W. E., 254
Godly Prayers 1559, 114–15
Gordon, General C., 259
Gore, Bp Charles, 341
Goudge, Elizabeth, 422
Goulburn, E. M., 267
Green, Peter, 402–3
Grey, Lady Jane, 64
Griffiths, Ann, 215
Grindal, Abp Edmund, 101
Guild of Saints Paul and Silas, 315
Gunning, Bp Peter, 146

Hale, Sir Matthew, 158
Hamilton, Bp Gavin, 128–30
Hamilton, Abp John, 100
Hammond, H., 156
Hare, Maria, 237
Hastings, Warren, 217
Havergal, Frances R., 284
Henry VI, King, 34
Henry VIII, King, household of, 59, 60
Henry, Matthew, 204
Hensley, L., 283
Herbert, George, 223–4
Herbert, Lady Lucy, 189
Herrick, Robert, 221–2
Hickes, Bp George, 199
Holben, D. M., 303
Holland, H. Scott, 333–4
Hollings, M., 427
Holy Year Prayer Book, 420
Hopkins, Gerard M., 304–5
Hort, F. J. A., 290
How, Bp William W., 287–8
Hume, Cardinal Basil, 426
Hunter, John, 335–6
Hymn-writers, prayers of, 279–84

Industrial Christian Fellowship, 384
Iona Books, 121
Ireland, Church of, 314, 316–17, 441–7
Ireland, Northern, 416–18

Jewell, Bp John, 77–8
Johnson, Samuel, 192–3
Jowett, J. H., 331–2
Julian of Norwich, 31

Keble, John, 298
Ken, Bp Thomas, 196–7
Kennedy, G. A. S., 375
Kerr, C., 416

King, Bp Edward, 292
Kingsley, Charles, 255–6
Knight, Prof W. A., 294–5
Knox, John, 75–6

Lambeth Conference 1930, 388
Lang, Abp Cosmo G., 359
Laud, Abp William, 140–2, 145
Law, William, 209
Leighton, Abp Robert, 159–61
Lewis, H. Elvet, 450
Liddon, H. P., 274–5
Lyte, H. F., 280
Lyttleton, Lord, 264

Macleod, N., 262
Macnutt, F. B., 365
Martin, Hugh, 412
Martin, Sir William, 247
Martineau, James, 246
Martyn, Henry, 232
Mary, Queen of Scots, 95
Matthews, W. R., 392
Maurice, F. D., 244
Maxwell, Prof J. Clark, 297
Meath, Earl of, 326
Methodist Church, 411
Milner-White, Eric, 393–5
Milton, John, 218
Montgomery, James, 279
More, Sir Thomas, 57
Morgan, Herbert, 448
Mothers' Union, 310, 405
Moule, Bp H. C. G., 329–30

Nairne, A., 357
Naylor, C. B., 408
Nelson, Horatio, Lord, 251
Newman, Prof F. W., 245
Newman, Cardinal J. H., 241–2, 299
Nicholas, W. Rhys, 178, 449, 451
Non-Jurors' Prayer Book, 214
Norwich Cathedral, 425

O'Brolechain, Maelishu, 25
Orchard, W. E., 372–3
Oxenham, John, 340

Paget, Bp F., 339
Parker, Abp Matthew, 99
Patrick, Bp P., 200
Patrick, St, 1–3
Penn, William, 201
Pilkington, Bp J., 61
Poets, prayers of, 218–30, 298–305
Prayer Book of 1928, 348–53
Presbyterian Church, Welsh, 453
Prichard, R., 178

Primers, Elizabethan, 104–5, 107, 111–13, 116, 119
Pusey, Edward B., 239–40

Raleigh, Sir Walter, 179
Ramsey, Abp Michael, 424
Ratcliffe, Prof E. C., 404
Recall to Religion, 389
Reformers, Protestant, 65–78
Reynolds, Bp Edward, 147
Rich, St Edmund, 29
Richard, St, 30
Ridding, Bp George, 291
Ridley, Bp Nicholas, 71
Robinson, Arthur W., 343–5
Robinson, J. Armitage, 354
Rolle, Richard, 33
Rossetti, Christina, 301–2

St Augustine's College, 390
Salisbury, Lord, 258
Sanderson, Bp Robert, 151
Scotland, Church of, 431–5
Scottish Episcopal Church, 436–40
Scottish Psalter 1595, 122–4
Shaftesbury, Lord, 253
Shakespeare, William, 180–1
Sheppard, H. R. L., 374
Sibbes, R., 139
Smith, Sir George A., 342
Smith, Bp J. Taylor, 356
Soulsby, L. H. M., 346–7
Southwell, Robert, 103
Sparrow, Bp Anthony, 171
Spenser, Edmund, 102
Stevenson, R. L., 260
Sumner, Mary, 310
Swift, Jonathan, 207–8

Tait, Abp Archibald C., 261
Taylor, Bp Jeremy, 162–9

Temple, Abp Frederick, 269–70
Temple, Abp William, 396–401
Tennyson, Alfred, Lord, 300
Thomas, John, 216
Thomas, Oliver, 177
Thomas, T. Glyn, 449
Thornhill, A. F., 312
Tillotson, Abp John, 174
Toc H Prayers, 382–3
Todd, J. M., 409
Traherne, Thomas, 194
Trench, Abp Richard C., 249
Tuttiett, L. R., 293
Tyndale, William, 66–7

Underhill, Evelyn, 371

Vaughan, C. J., 263
Vaughan, Henry, 226
Vicars, Capt Hedley, 289

Wales, Church in, 387, 452
War-time prayers, forms of, 376–81
Watts, Isaac, 227
Welsh Methodist Church, 386
Wesley, Charles, 228
Wesley, John, 190–1
Westcott, Bp B. Foss, 320–5
Westminster Confession of Faith, 176
White, H. Kirk, 235
William III, King, 187–8
Williams, Rowland, 265–6
Williams, William, 211
Wilson, Bp Thomas, 205–6
Wither, George, 143–4
Woods, Bp F. T., 366
Wooton, Sir Henry, 131
Wordsworth, Bp John, 306

Yelverton, Sir Christopher, 120

Index of Subjects

Adversity, 266
Afflicted, the, 28, 146, 168, 175, 294
Agriculture, 361
Aid, divine, 57, 181
All conditions of men, 146
All Saints, 83
Andrew, St, 89
Armada, the, 97
Armed forces, 378
Arts, the, 434–5
Aspiration, 8, 9
Atomic power, 365
Authority, those in, 66, 129, 338

Benedictions, 51, 54, 67, 86, 330, 353, 401
Bible, 202, 342; see also Word of God
Bidding prayer, 126
Birthday, 23
Bishops, 11
Blind, the, 343
British Empire, 326
Brotherhood, 433

Carefulness, against, 117
Carpenter, Jesus, Master, 383
Chaplains, service, 356
Cheerfulness, 238, 346
Childbirth, 327
Children, 12, 155, 169, 195, 405
Christ:
    coming of, 152, 214
    kingship of, 143
    mind of, 69
    Saviour, the, 257, 302
    Son of God, 300
    Spirit of, 340
    Teacher, the, 242
Christmas, 82, 413
Church:
    national, 106, 452
    parochial, 402
    universal, 75–6, 119, 133, 141, 163, 362, 424, 448
Class distinctions, 329
Clergy, the, 92, 275, 403
Commendations, 29, 136, 181
Commitment to Christ, 62, 99
Commonwealth, the, 368
Communion of Saints, 335, 432
Compassion, 407, 424

Confession of sin, 87
Consecration, 233, 284
Contentment, 272
Conversion, 420
Conviction, 71
Covenant Service, Methodist, 411
Creation, 7, 36, 297
Cross:
    appeal of the, 270
    remembrance of, 289
    see also Passion

Death, 195, 230
Dedication, 27, 53, 105, 160, 189, 191, 233–4, 284, 358, 400, 411, 423
Departed, the, 84, 108, 134, 201, 269, 290, 352
Discipleship, 104
Doxologies, 137, 196, 430

Easter, 102
Education, 350
Eisteddfod, National, 385
Election, general, 341
Enemies, 380
Epiphany, 152, 439
Eternal, things, 369
Evangelism, 285, 292
Evening, 110
Evening of life, 280
Evil and good, 17

Faith, 59, 72, 77, 107, 198–9, 296, 300
Faithfulness, 165, 234, 255, 259, 291
Family, the, 261, 316, 386, 404
Farmers, 361
Fears, our, 450
Fellowship, 249
Fisheries, 440
Forgiveness, God's, 33, 45, 56, 206
Freedom, spiritual, 95
Friends, 167, 247, 261, 328
Fruits of the earth, 153

Generosity, 248, 308, 336
George, St, 306
Gifts, God's, 35, 112, 447
Gloria, 78, 430
God:
    debtors to, 27
    eternal, 13

238

supreme, 19, 31
Grace, 135, 222
Gratitude, 35, 224, 332; *see also*
Thanksgivings
Guidance, 131, 278, 344

Harvest, 52, 153, 314
Health, 154, 157
Heaven, 5, 46, 138, 299
Holiness, 101, 156, 164, 171, 185, 219,
229
Holy Communion, 170, 176, 254, 282,
305, 395, 431
Holy Spirit, 115, 150, 453
Home and family life, 40, 310
Homes, broken, 444
Hospitals, 319
House of Commons, 120
Humility, 256, 287, 301
Hunger, world, 406

Incarnation, 103
Industries, 351
Intercessions, 159, 347
Invocations, 6, 25, 116, 311
Ireland, 416–18, 441–7

Jealousy, 295
Jews, 312
Joy, 48
Judge, God the, 218
Judgment-seat, 438
Justice, administration of, 68, 354

Kingdom of God, 178, 205, 283, 293,
363, 394
Knowledge of God, 74, 235, 245,
318

Law, offenders against the, 161
Leaders, Church, 388
Life:
our daily, 38, 172, 182, 192, 204,
264, 317
sanctity of, 139, 446
the Christian, 185–6, 204, 225, 317,
334, 414
Light, spiritual, 4, 65, 113, 138, 273,
392
Love:
for God, 73, 111, 194, 209, 321
for others, 130, 217, 324, 427–8

Margaret, St, 436
Marriage, 310
Mary, Virgin, 304, 413
Media, 435
Mental health, 408, 422
Mercy, for, 22

Ministry, the ordained, 148–9, 271,
274
Missions, 279, 313, 349, 364, 373, 443
Morning, 109, 203, 236, 260
Mothers, 310
Music, 360

Nation, the, 96, 132, 140, 162, 258,
333, 367, 389, 442
Nations, 32, 123, 125, 396
Navy, Royal, 151
Need, those in, *see* Afflicted
New Year, 372

Ordination, before, 359; *see also*
Ministry
Overseas, the Church, *see* Missions

Parish, 268, 403
Parliament, 120, 145
Passion, Christ's, 225, 270, 289
Patrick, St, 441
Peace:
industrial, 398
inward, 42, 54, 80, 231, 237, 240,
320, 346, 371, 446
mutual, 124, 445
world, 339, 355, 370, 381, 393,
429
Penitence, *see* Repentance
Pentecost, 309, 437; *see also* Holy
Spirit
Perseverance, 3
Petitions, personal, 1–2, 26, 49, 142,
179, 219, 303, 375
Pilgrimage, life's, 210–11
Poverty, world, 406
Praise, 50, 100, 121–2, 158, 200, 227,
281, 298, 451
Prayer, 44, 93, 126, 207–8, 220–1,
250
Presence, God's, 58, 226, 371
Prisoners of war, 379
Prisons, 315
Protection, 10, 18, 37, 41, 75
Providence, 61
Purity, 33

Queen, the, 91; *see also* Sovereign

Racial unity, 382
Reconciliation, 419
Refuge, God our, 105
Religions, other, 409
Renewal, spiritual, 410
Repentance, 15, 70, 229
Responsibility, our, 390
Resurrection, 102
Rich, the, 286

Saints, All, 83
Saints of our nation, 348, 357
Schools, *see* Education
Scriptures, *see* Word of God
Servants, God's, 14, 255
Service, Christian, 190, 223, 239, 253,
    277, 313
Sickness, 157
Sincerity, 216
Single-mindedness, 243
Social justice, 183, 322, 397, 425
Soldier's prayer, a, 127
Sovereign, the, 24, 187, 213
Steadfastness, 166
Suffering, our, 241
Supplications, 20, 22, 43, 215, 449,
    453
Sympathy, 374

Temptation, 118
Thanksgivings, 30, 35, 100, 147, 314,
    447
Time, passage of, 192, 246
Tongue, the, 47
Travellers, 391
Trinity, Holy, 39, 244, 307, 449

Trouble, in times of, 79, 263, 266
Truth, 325, 345

Understanding, spiritual, 21
Unemployed, the, 384
Unity:
    Christian, 212, 244, 415
    Church, 114, 197, 399
    Class, 249, 323
    National, 366
Usefulness, 262, 265

Victory, national, 98, 251
Vision of God, 16

Wales:
    Church in, 452
    people of, 177, 387
War, in time of, 88, 337, 355, 376–7
Warfare, Christian, 144
Will of God, 34, 64, 186
Word of God, 60, 63, 81, 202; *see also*
    Bible
Work, our, 193, 252, 267, 331
Worship, 85, 94, 276

Zeal, renewed, 288